BEACH
HOUSES
OF SOUTH AMERICA

Shortly after obtaining one of the most interesting projects
featured in this publication—Cavaco's House in Angra dos Reis,
Rio de Janeiro—Sylvia Haidar, the South American representative of
The Images Publishing Group, received sad news. The architect
Cláudio Bernardes had been fatally injured in an accident and had
passed away, far from home while visiting one of his client's projects.
This book is dedicated to him.

BEACH
HOUSES
OF SOUTH AMERICA

images
Publishing

Published in Australia in 2003 by
The Images Publishing Group Pty Ltd
ACN 059 734 431
6 Bastow Place, Mulgrave, Victoria 3170, Australia
Telephone (61 3) 9561 5544 Facsimile (61 3) 9561 4860
E-mail: books@images.com.au
Website: www.imagespublishinggroup.com

National Library of Australia Cataloguing-in-Publication Data

Haidar, Sylvia
Beach Houses of South America

ISBN: 1 87690 782 7

1. Architecture, Domestic—South America.
2. Seaside Architecture—South America. I. Title.

728.098

Co-ordinating Editors: Jodie Davis and Sarah Noal
Designed by The Graphic Image Studio Pty Ltd, Mulgrave, Australia
Film separations by Mission Productions Ltd., Hong Kong
Printed by Everbest Printing Co. Ltd. in Hong Kong/China

CONTENTS

INTRODUCTION

As the South American representative of The Images Publishing Group, Sylvia Haidar has been instrumental in introducing the work of major South American architects to an international audience.

When planning *Beach Houses of South America,* Haidar was faced with a choice: to define a clear architectural theme for the chosen projects or to use a more flexible approach, which highlighted different, contemporary South American architectural styles.

Surrounded by vast oceans, South America embodies the convergence of ideas from both the east and the west. Since its colonization, the continent has been open to new influences linked to traditional and modern concepts, the latter verging at times on 'kitsch.' Its huge, diverse population consists of people from all over the world, who have brought with them entrenched habits and strong memories of the lands they left behind.

South America can be divided into two distinct parts. Spanish South America is composed of many countries with the same written and spoken language and a similar culture. The Portuguese South America of Brazil is a vast country, as big as a continent, rich in natural resources and wide spaces but with many social contradictions. Nevertheless, despite social disparity, great poverty and considerable violence, the countries of South America have still managed to transform many of these obstacles into creative resources.

Given such rich and complex cultural diversities, Haidar believed that a flexible approach was most appropriate for this publication. Her research examined different architectonic resources—some contemporary, some traditional—but always with a focus on the latest developments in construction and architecture worldwide, and always mindful of local culture.

The houses and locations presented in *Beach Houses of South America* are just as varied as the cultures of South America. They range from the arid and wild environment of the Pacific coast to the warm, tropical climate of the Atlantic coasts. The houses range from weekend getaways to family homes. They are a way of life for some South Americans and the ocean, sand and forests are integral to that way of life.

The continent's coastline has a long and varied coastal history. Centuries before European discovery, the indigenous South Americans made their living from the abundant produce of the oceans. The coastline was also the location of the earliest colonizers' fortresses built to protect against piracy and invasion. Later, commercial sites flourished as trade with Europe grew. Now, these sites serve a different purpose—the beaches are wonderful locations for local and foreign tourism and the surrounding forests are preserved to protect the existing fauna and flora.

In compiling this book, Haidar would like to thank a number of people for their assistance, in particular all the architects involved and without whom this book would not exist. Also, many thanks to the architect and artist Franz Krajcberg who kindly allowed the inclusion of his unique Tree House in this publication.

Haidar is indebted to those who introduced her to some of the architects featured in this book—Hilda Araújo Bratke, Laura Braun e Silva and Ruth Salem Sader from São Paulo, Brazil, Suzana Chaves Barcellos from Rio Grande do Sul, Brazil, and Magdalena Giuria from Buenos Aires, Argentina.

Thanks to all the photographers whose superb photographs appear in this book, notably, Nelson Kon (Felix Beach House, Marcos Acayaba House and Casa Baeta), Rômulo Fialdini (Gamboa House), Célio Alves Rodrigues Jr (who worked with Haidar in Trancoso) and Márcio Scavone (who introduced her to Franz Krajcberg).

Haidar's special thanks go to Bruce Anthony Harris for his emotional and technical (English revision) support.

BRAZIL

BRAZIL

The largest country in South America, Brazil is home to a great variety of coastal enclaves, from Guarujá in the southeast to Ceará, in the northeast.

The areas featured here are among the most beautiful in the country, and the homes situated on these beaches reflect the laid-back, peaceful seaside life.

The Brazilian coast has a rich history of pirate invasions, smuggling, trading, colonial settlement, indigenous habitation, and fishing— and when combined with the natural wonders of the waterfalls, mountains, wildlife, and lagoons, it all makes for a vibrant and visually spectacular environment.

The areas of Brazil featured here are:

- the Alagoas Coast
- Uruaú Lagoon, Beberibe in Ceará
- Guarujá, São Sebastião, Ilha Bela and Ubatuba in São Paulo
- Praia do Toquinho/Ipojuca in Pernambuco
- Itaparica Island, Nova Viçosa and Trancoso in Bahia
- Armação de Búzios, Angra do Reis, Laranjeiras' Beach, and Ilha Grande in Rio de Janeiro
- Pingo d'Água Beach, Ilha Grande

HOUSE IN ALTO DO SEGREDO
TRANCOSO • BAHIA • BRAZIL

RICARDO SALEM AND BEATRIZ REGIS BITTENCOURT

Alto do Segredo, one of Trancoso's most fabulous beaches, shelters these two houses, which are built on the same land in the same form and arrangement. The only differences lie in the colors and interior decoration. The owners, two sisters, live in harmony with their families and friends during holidays and weekends, and coexist happily thanks to the private areas and wide open community spaces. At the entrance, there is a garage on one side, and the tenant's house and the laundry on the other.

With an exuberant flowering garden, the walk to the main house features many exotic and tropical local plants. The main house faces the glorious natural surrounds, while the kitchen and dining room form a point of union between each family's private living areas. On the ground level, there is a large veranda on one side and the rooms for the children and the guests. The master bedroom takes up most of the first level out to a balcony with a perfect sea view, and also features a closet and bathroom.

The materials used are all local, with the choice of timber being influenced by a strong sense of ecological responsibility. The roof and some of the creative furniture were made especially for this house by Ricardo.

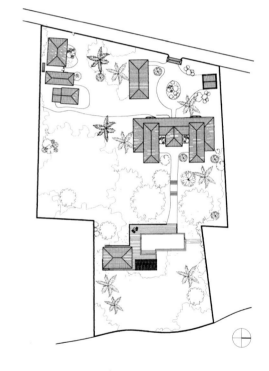

top: site plan

right: entire block and surroundings

opposite top: front view of house from swimming pool

opposite bottom: detail of side façade with balcony on upper level and open living area on ground level

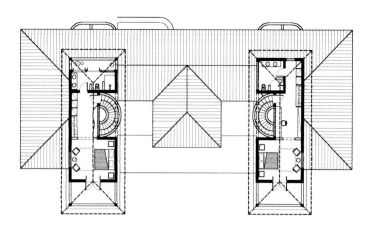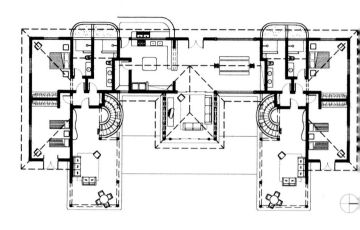

HOUSE IN ALTO DO SEGREDO

top left: upper level floor plan

top right: lower level floor plan

above: side detail of façade with tropical vegetation

opposite top left: floor plan for tenant's house and laundry

opposite top left middle: dog kennel and storage

opposite top right middle : swimming pool and surrounding area

opposite top right: children's house—not built

opposite middle right: view to ocean from upper level

opposite middle left: barbecue and deck

opposite bottom: guest bedroom on ground level with bed designed by Ricardo Salem

photographer: Célio Alves Rodrigues Jr

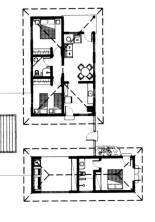

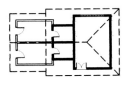

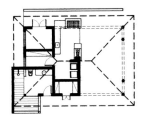

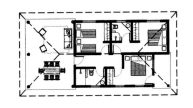

ARCHITECT'S HOUSE IN BÚZIOS

ARMAÇÃO DE BÚZIOS•RIO DE JANEIRO•BRAZIL

OCTÁVIO RAJA GABAGLIA

This house is set in dense vegetation in an area of 63,000 square meters (678,132 square feet) in Ponta da Sapata, Búzios, and boasts one of the world's most beautiful treasures—nature itself. Taking full advantage of the land's excellent location and its aerial view to the sea and surrounding beaches, architect Octávio Raja Gabaglia designed his own house to focus on the features of the beautiful region and the original habitat.

The house, located on the most escarped point of the land with a 270-degree view of the sea, required integrated construction with native vegetation. The architect's challenges were many. Choosing a very narrow escarpment of land, 20 meters (65 feet) at the widest point and 25 meters (82 feet) above sea level, the house had to be sized to fit exactly into the area. With a narrow modulation of 5 meters (16 feet) on the entire house (except for the verandas which are 3.2 meters (10.5 feet) wide) the problem was solved.

The construction has two notable characteristics: it snakes around the terrain while allowing for the existing trees, and assumes perfect integration with the environment.

Different levels also made this integration with the land easy and, at the same time, allowed a fantastic play of different roof heights and openings strategically taking advantage of the dominant winds to provide perfect ventilation in all conditions.

Quite intentionally, the house has a very simple façade and, from the parking area, appears half-buried, increasing the strong surprise effect created by the view of the sea on leaving the entrance hall.

The use of a wide range of natural materials—local stone for the walls, hand-cut wood for the structure, columns and roof, second-hand ceramics obtained from demolished old colonial houses for the roof, and extensive use of glass— all represent the singular style of this unique architect. Gabaglia's architectonic focus also created the perfect integration of the interior and exterior. His influence was felt initially in Búzios and subsequently spread to other parts of the country.

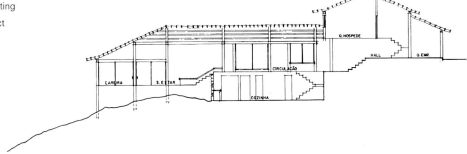

right top: aerial view; location of house's stone walls allows the building to blend with local vegetation

right bottom: section

opposite: view from swimming pool to ocean

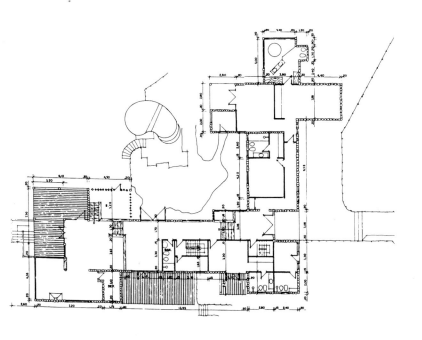

ARCHITECT'S **HOUSE** IN **BÚZIOS**

opposite: view of lower level

top left: view of upper level

middle: wooden structure of hall

left: site plan

above: view of lower level

photographers: J D Tardioli and Paulinho Muniz

BEACH **HOUSE** ON **THE** HILL **I**

IPORANGA/GUARUJÁ•SÃO PAULO•BRAZIL

NELSON DUPRÉ

Situated only 300 meters (984 feet) from the sea and 120 meters (406 feet) up in the Serra do Mar, this beautiful house exists in a very special location. The use of natural materials complements the surroundings, and the transparency of the rooms provides excellent views of the beach, hills, and forest. The house takes advantage of its position and environment to remain fresh and ventilated during summer, and warm and pleasant in winter.

The pronounced slope of the land allows the use of a platform design that guarantees absolute privacy for the lower level bedrooms and gives the master bedroom, which faces the ocean, a close integration with the surroundings.

The communal area on the upper level allows for a view of the landscape across the Atlantic Forest treetops and straight to the ocean. The open mezzanine floor, which adjoins the communal area, affords the owner, an international consultant, both an astonishing view as well as the peace and calm necessary for his work.

Nelson Dupré, making use of natural materials such as wood, stone, clay, and especially glass, had as his main objective the integration of the house with the surrounding environment and the garden, which preserves the land's original trees.

top: swimming pool

right: main entrance; elevation northwest

opposite: main entrance

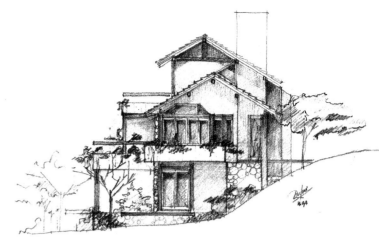

BEACH **HOUSE** ON **THE** HILL **I**
opposite top: sketch
opposite bottom: main access and garden
top: mezzanine balcony
middle: office view from mezzanine
above: master bathroom

23

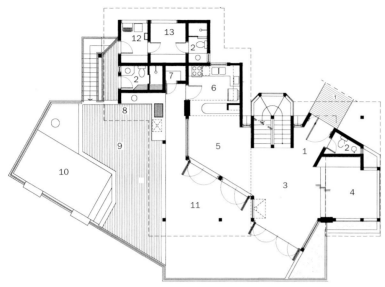

1   entrance
2   bathroom
3   living
4   games room
5   dining
6   kitchen
7   pantry
8   barbecue
9   deck
10 swimming pool
11 terrace
12 laundry
13 tenant's room

1   hall/stair
2   double bedroom
3   single bedroom
4   master bedroom
5   bathroom
6   closet
7   bathroom
8   tenant's living and kitchen
9   tenant's bedroom
10 garage
11 deck

0   3ft

BEACH HOUSE ON THE HILL I

top: ground level

above: lower level

right: stair

opposite top: living room

opposite bottom left: dining room and mezzanine

opposite bottom right: comfortable furnishings in games room

photographer: Nelson Dupré

BEACH **HOUSE** ON **THE** HILL **II**
ILHA BELA•SÃO SEBASTIÃO•SÃO PAULO•BRAZIL

NELSON DUPRÉ

The house was built 400 meters (1312 feet) from the ocean and 100 meters (328 feet) up the southern slope of Ilha Bela, facing the channel that separates the island from the mainland. Its design was based on Nelson Dupré's main architectural principles for leisure residences: total integration with the environment and the use of natural materials, especially glass.

The communal area, on the same level as the main entrance, is surrounded by a large balcony and faces west over the forest. The service areas—the kitchen, barbecue, and so on—are located closer to the street creating a very intimate living area. The bedrooms are situated on the lower level, linked by a large terrace facing the ocean.

The nature of the construction methods and materials used made for the easy execution of work, helped keep the cost low, and, very importantly, helped to integrate the house with the environment.

With his great respect for nature and the land, Dupré designed this house most effectively, positioning it among trees and building it over the land's rock formation. The house's integration with the surrounding environment and the Atlantic Forest microclimate provide a sense of calm as one faces the sun setting over the ocean.

opposite top: bay window of dining room

opposite bottom: barbecue; elevation northwest

top left: west elevation

top right: south elevation

above: main entrance; elevation northeast

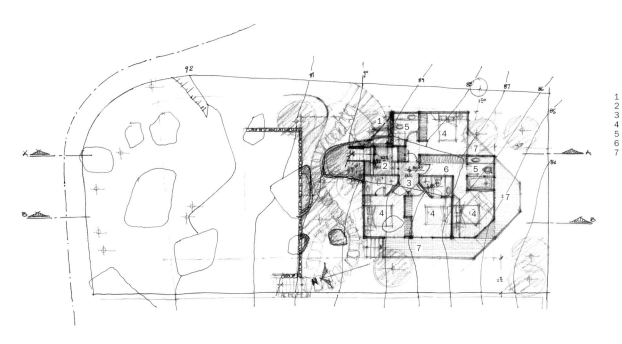

1   main entrance
2   access hall
3   hall to bedrooms
4   single bedroom
5   bathroom
6   closet
7   deck

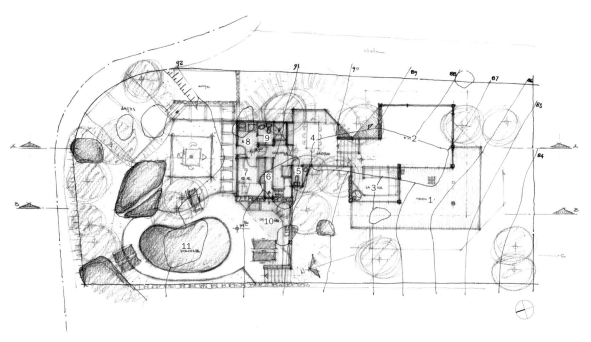

1   terrace
2   living room
3   fireplace
4   dining room
5   toilet
6   kitchen
7   servant's room
8   service area
9   bathroom
10 barbecue
11 swimming pool

BEACH **HOUSE** ON **THE** HILL II

top: site plan; ground level

above: site plan; upper level

right: sunset view facing ocean from living room balcony

opposite top left: circulation/dining room (internal view)

opposite top right: ground level; bedrooms' terrace/upper level living room balcony

opposite bottom left: living room

opposite bottom right: living room balcony

photographer: Nelson Dupré

CASA BAETA, IPORANGA
GUARUJÁ • SÃO PAULO • BRAZIL

MARCOS ACAYABA

On an area of 1200 square meters (12,917 square feet) with a strong upward incline from the street to the backyard, this work had a number of construction challenges such as the fragility of the land and the difficulty of storing building materials. However, the architect's greatest challenge was how to build in such a way as to preserve the natural vegetation and at the same time avoid land movement.

Considering the land's position at the base of a mountain, close to the Atlantic Forest and facing the sea, Marcos Acayaba designed this residence taking the best aspects of the structural potential of timber. He opted for a triangular mesh supporting the house with six reinforced concrete pillars. From each pillar, six 'French Hands' emerge, appearing as six hexagons. This allowed the residence to be 'freed' from the earth, and vegetation and rainwater to pass freely under the construction. This rigid, undistorted structure and the natural auto locking determined the layout of its internal spaces and allowed for the possibility of growth in the construction. Thus, the first challenge was met and resolved.

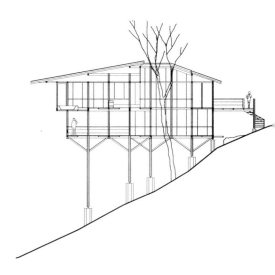

However, storing building materials and providing shelter for workers continued to be a problem. The solution was to use industrialized and light materials. The building parts were all made in a factory and most of them were made out of small pieces of wood, allowing quick local assembly. There was no need for heavy materials and three workers did the work in 40 days.

Two levels set around a courtyard arranged the internal spaces so that all areas have a view of the sea. This was one result of the triangular modulation, which increased the views. The hexagonal and open courtyard ensured the preservation of two large native trees, which reach up to the sky through the centre of the house.

On the lower level, the kitchen and living room are perfectly integrated with a covered terrace facing the ocean. On the upper level, four bedrooms sit beside each other, with a wooden deck facing the forest. Made in the shape of a ship's prow, the master bedroom projects itself from the trees into the landscape.

The broken and hexagonal nature of the construction blends with the vegetation and the building merges into its natural surroundings.

top: section

right: main entrance; view of deck and stair facing forest

opposite: house immersed in surrounding forest

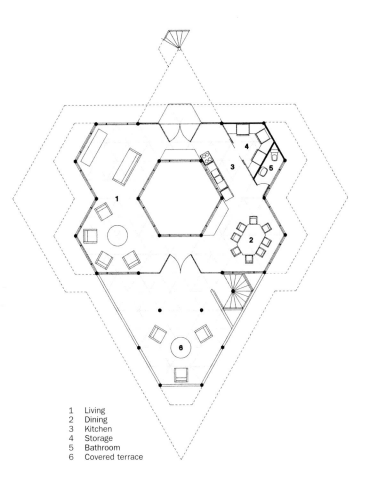

1 Living
2 Dining
3 Kitchen
4 Storage
5 Bathroom
6 Covered terrace

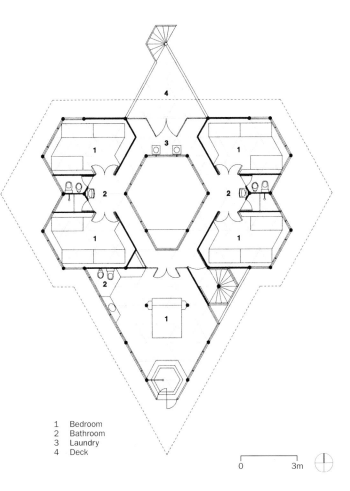

1 Bedroom
2 Bathroom
3 Laundry
4 Deck

0 ————— 3m

CASA BAETA, IPORANGA

opposite: internal courtyard

top: house supported by wooden supports

above left: lower floor plan; kitchen, living and covered terrace

above right: upper floor plan; bedrooms

CASA BAETA, IPORANGA

top: internal view of house

right: master bedroom with jacuzzi facing ocean

opposite: internal view of house

CASA BAETA, IPORANGA
opposite: covered terrace by evening
left: steel cable
above: view from wooden supports
photographer: Nelson Kon

37

CASA **BRAVA**
PRAIA BRAVA DA FORTALEZA•UBATUBA•SÃO PAULO•BRAZIL

LÍLIAN AND RENATO DAL PIAN

This summerhouse, located in Praia Brava da Fortaleza, was built on a declivity lot of 9000 square meters and is bordered by the exuberant vegetation of the Mata Atlântica and the ocean.

The design concept paid attention to the hot and humid climate and to the difficulty of transporting materials to the site.

The house is composed of two prefabricated wooden pavilions on a structure of two cement slab floors so that the building remains completely isolated within the lot.

The roof is divided by three planes of aluminum tiles that protect the house from the strong and constant rain during summertime, while also providing the interior with a continuous supply of fresh air through large openings.

The 'two pavilions' concept, linked by stairs, allows a distinct separation between the living and common areas. The lower first pavilion is where the living room and kitchen are located and opens on to a spacious veranda through large glass doors. The upper second pavilion contains the bedrooms, which look out onto the beautiful landscapes of the ocean and the lush flora. The roof lamina and the continuum bank protect and define the veranda, providing a gentle horizontal aspect to the house that is interrupted by the transversal access stairway and by two vertical masonry structures holding the barbecue and the wood stove, two mainstays of traditional Brazilian cooking.

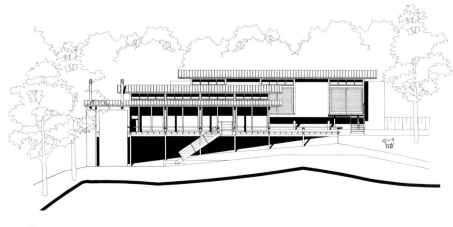

opposite left: frontal elevation

opposite right: view of house with surrounding flora

top left: front façade of common area pavilion

top right: general view—terrace (common area pavilion) and bedroom stair (private pavilion)

above: view of deck

39

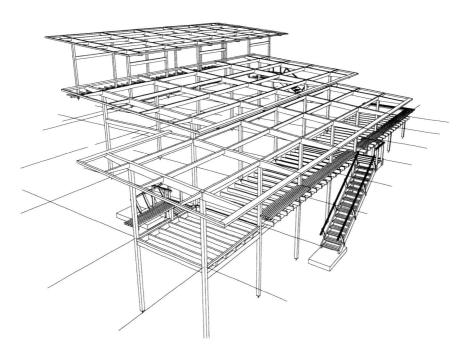

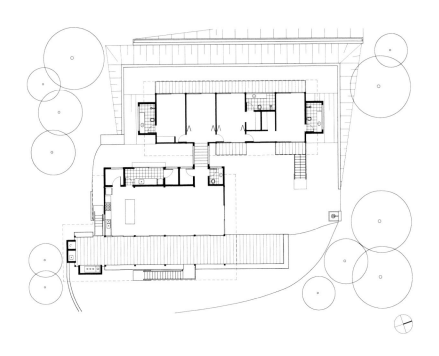

CASA**BRAVA**

opposite top: wooden structural system

opposite bottom: bedroom view—private pavilion

top right: site plan

top left: view of living room and terrace

above: view of barbecue and wood stove from terrace

left: night view of dining room

photographers: Lilian and Renato Dal Pian

CAVACO'S HOUSE
ANGRA DOS REIS•RIO DE JANEIRO•BRAZIL

CLÁUDIO BERNARDES AND PAULO JACOBSEN

This house, designed by the Cláudio Bernardes and Paulo Jacobsen studio, is located on Cavaco Island, one of the 365 islands in the Angra dos Reis region. The project's position on the island is determined by many things. On one side, there are the sinuous lines of the site's plan that follow the level curves of the original land and thus set the house into the topography. On the other side, the orientation of the house directly toward the dominant, strong southwest winds requires a completely sealed construction.

The total compound is made up of several different blocks: the swimming pool and its surroundings, the main house, and the belvedere where there are three guest bungalows.

The swimming pool pavilion is shaded using *piaçava*, a native name for a palm tree fiber, which flows out from a large central mast, and features a variation in height that forms a caracole.

The main house has two levels. The upper level, containing two wide suites, is framed by a large veranda with a grassy flagstone and has a complete view of the surroundings. On one side, there is a 28-meter-long (92-foot) ramp that links the two bedrooms and leads to an internal garden through a glass opening under a concrete pergola.

The wide social areas of the ground level are linked by the same ceramic floor and also face the surrounding landscape, bringing the sinuous lines of the adjacent mountains to the interior space and blending harmoniously with the project lines.

The construction is free from the land's slope allowing a large overture on the back of the main living area, which generates natural and cross-ventilation. A very large tree was used as a poetic element between the big veranda, the main living room, and the upper floor, stretching out from the house's outer limits to the sky.

The materials used in the construction (steel, glass, and concrete) were meant to give lightness to the overall house through smooth lines and wide openings. The concrete pillars are covered with copper and are still too new to be a perfect match with the surroundings but this will come with aging. They support the grassy flagstones as a suspended garden, forming large terraces. Brennand ceramic tiles on the floor replicate the bottom of the ocean and the line of grassy flagstone forms a perfect line with Angra's geography.

The internal ambience is created by using natural materials that oppose the materials used for the construction itself. The unifying feature is the blue tone of the construction, which makes the blue of the sky and the ocean appear as a compliment to the creativity of the architects.

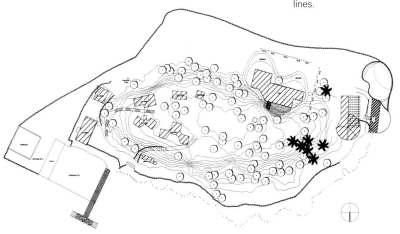

above: master plan of island

opposite top: frontal aerial view of house

opposite bottom: view of veranda's living room, with stair in *pedra costeira* (coast stone) that leads to swimming pool; pillars are covered with new copper

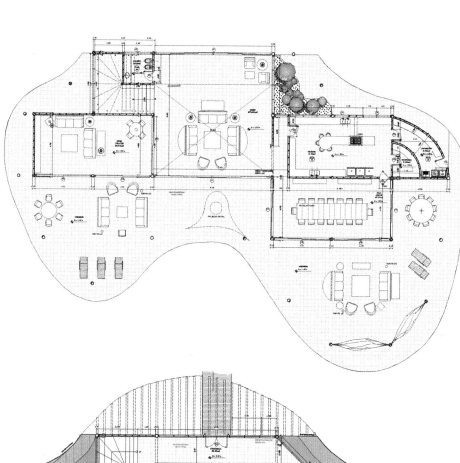

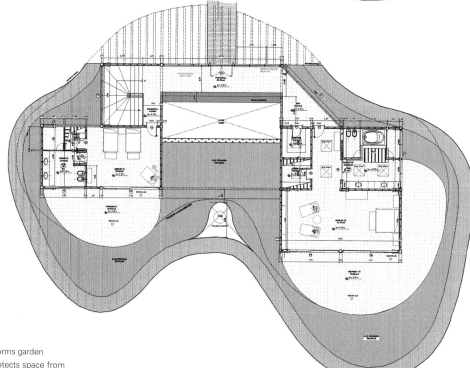

CAVACO'S HOUSE

top: circulation ramp between bedrooms; left, natural terrain forms garden protected by white aluminum framework; right, steel bench protects space from lower level; concrete and glass pergola covers whole circulation ramp

middle: lower level floor plan

right: upper level floor plan

opposite: view from top of island of sinuous line, which changes depending on viewer's angle.

CAVACO'S HOUSE

above: master bedroom on upper level

right: pool pavilion with wood and palm-fiber cover
forming caracole

opposite: living room

photographer: Kitty Paranaguá

ESTRELA DO MAR HOUSE
ALAGOAS COAST•ALAGOAS•BRAZIL

HUMBERTA FARIAS

Together with Olga Wanderley, architect Humberta Farias designed this house on 2000 square meters (21,528 square feet) of land, surrounded by an ecological reserve. On one side there is a coconut tree jungle and, on the other, a large native swamp.

Using her main style characteristics—regionalism mixed with modern—Humberta designed the house's structure in concrete and used local materials for the exterior and interior finishes. Thus, the wooden roof is covered with clay tile, rushes are found in many parts of the house and the bricks are largely from the local area.

Using the 'sea star' as inspiration, the house forms a clear geometric volume with defined lines, and this shows up in the surrounding context. The house is divided into two different blocks, the main body featuring two floors and a leisure area surrounding the swimming pool.

The main access is on the swamp side together with the swimming pool area,. This is completed by a sauna, kitchen aid, a barbecue area, the service area, and the shade for the swimming pool and the garages.

The main block is 450 square meters (4845 square feet) where the ground floor provides the social areas, which are distributed throughout a large and wide saloon. A common and informal meeting place, characterized by a brightly colored Brazilian fabric motif, can be found on the middle floor. The bedrooms are on the upper floor. They share the mezzanine's large hall where there are stairs and a connection from the lower level to the upper level.

Everything was planned to lessen the impact of Alagoas' warm weather. Many rooms are designed in a way to receive the region's prevailing winds and to take advantage of the sunsets.

Humberta Farias shows particular flair for interior design and makes a special effort to include the region's crafts in her designs, involving the creative talents of the local people.

One can see in this house the architect's principal characteristics, the concern for incorporating the landscape, and attention to the client's satisfaction.

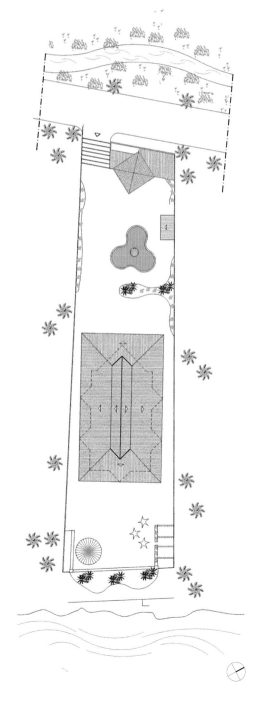

right: site plan
opposite: west façade

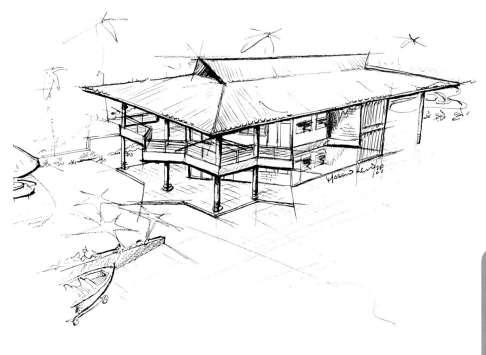

ESTRELA DO MAR HOUSE

opposite: east façade and leisure area

top: perspective

above: west façade

left: deck detail

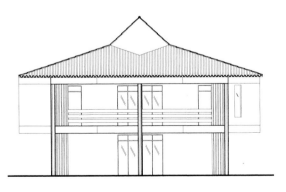

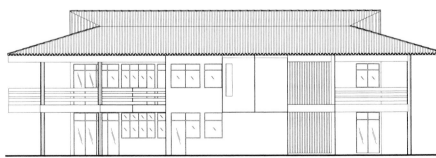

ESTRELA DO MAR HOUSE

top left: view of west façade by moonlight

top right: detail of south façade

above left: west façade

above right: south façade

opposite: view from upper level balcony to ocean

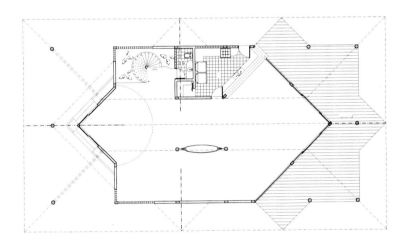

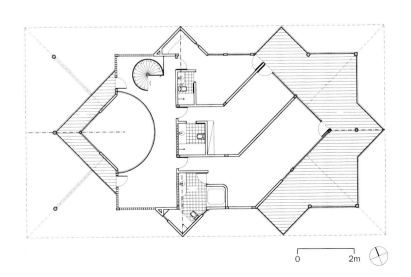

0   2m

57

FELIX BEACH HOUSE
PRAIA DO FELIX•SÃO PAULO•BRAZIL

ANNE MARIE SUMNER

Felix House, located at beautiful Felix Beach, appears as a floating plaza in the midst of treetops.

When she first chose the orientation of the house, Anne Marie Sumner took advantage of the strong declivity of the lot, common in the Ubatuba region, and designed a geometric sectioned block where the volume emphasized the contrast between the built object and the surrounding natural environment.

The structure is made of reinforced concrete on two levels, alternating opacity and solidity with transparency and lightness.

The house is supported by consoles attached to the native rocks by long iron rods. The lack of visible pillars and beams creates a simple and distinctive form.

On the lower level, a corridor, which opens all the way to the landscape, is a natural frame for the bedrooms. On the upper level, a large veranda, which shelters the dining and living rooms, projects straight out to the horizontal air space.

The use of simple and noble materials is a good example of economy, a touch the architect likes to emphasize.

Without decorative elements to establish its identity, the house can be seen as a quest for interior/exterior integration and the organization of a universe of references without any natural elements. Its tranquility and the uniformity of the materials provide a well of silence allowing one to transcend the substantive construction and attain a deeper sense of human life.

opposite left: view into house

opposite right: Prussian blue of house against backdrop of jungle and beach

top left: all windows frame ocean

top right: steel parapets create a theme with sea rollers

above: night view of house

FELIX BEACH HOUSE

opposite: 'cut' into floor conceals internal stairway linking
bedrooms with living area

top: terrace in the evening

above: view from master bedroom

left: native rock is integrated into house's design

photographer: Nelson Kon

61

GAMBOA HOUSE

GAMBOA BEACH•ITAPARICA ISLAND•BAHIA•BRAZIL

DAVID BASTOS

With a privileged view of Todos os Santos Bay, this house faithfully represents the architecture of David Bastos— wide-open spaces, white, and not too dense where the natural light plays an integral role.

Built in juxtaposed modules, linked by the circulation, the house has been designed to include two floors. On the top floor are the bedrooms. The master bedroom boasts a terrace with a lovely view to the ocean, and a transparent polycarbonate roof to let in the natural light. On the lower floor, the communal rooms are located with an open view to the exterior. The steel stairs seem like a sculpture that gently fills the space.

The house was built for a young couple who wanted a practical and functional space in which to enjoy holidays with family and friends. Fifty-three days were spent on construction. The widespread use of sliding windows; a very low parapet that takes advantage of the fantastic landscape; and the choice of one single stone material for the floors in all rooms, all helped facilitate the quick construction.

The cross-ventilation encouraged by the open windows, together with the constant breeze on the northeast Brazilian beaches, provides fresh and ventilated air throughout the house.

There is a mix of natural materials in the interior design: sisal carpets, natural fiber tables and chairs, wood for the entrance door, and high-tech materials for the decks and sideboards. This combination, together with the best modern technological comforts (such as remote control doors, venetian blinds, and a machine to pick up the boat from the ocean) shows David Bastos understands the Brazilian way of life in the global context.

From any part of the house, the view is wide—on one side a grove of coconut trees, on another, wooden decking built over a stream, facing the green slope of the land. At the front is the beautiful swimming pool that looks out to the drama of the sea.

top: view from coconut grove—clear view of construction in juxtaposed modules

above & opposite: front view of house

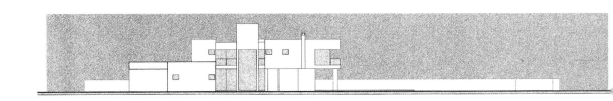

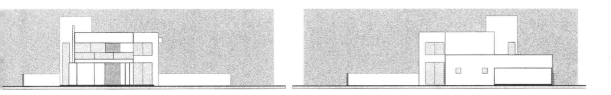

opposite top: southwest façade

opposite bottom: swimming pool decking facing sea

top left: northeast façade

top right: southeast façade

above: master bedroom's wooden decking; timber door in *ipê-Tabaçu*; Todos os Santos Bay in distance and city of Salvador beyond

left: wooden decking built over stream

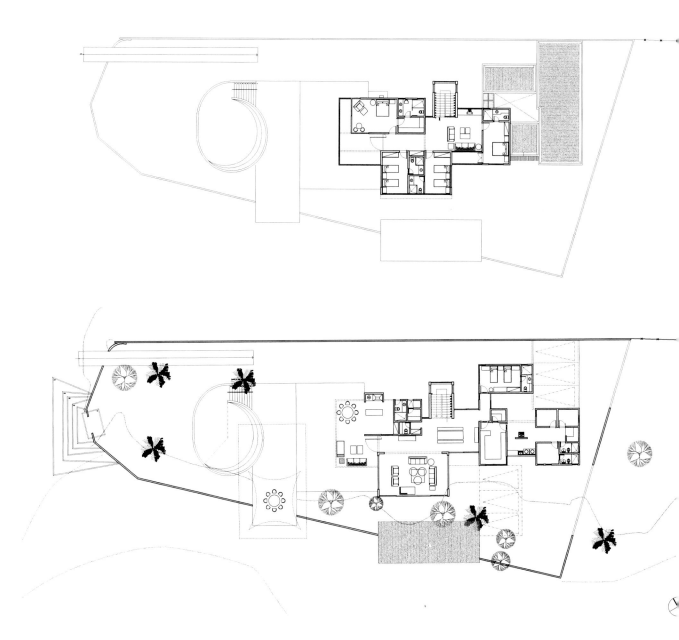

GAMBOA HOUSE

top: circulation corridor to terrace ensures privacy for master bedroom;
metallic structure roof made from transparent polycarbonate

middle: upper level floor plan

bottom: lower level floor plan

opposite: view from living room to garden

GAMBOAHOUSE

opposite: dining room and stairs

top: master bedroom with terrace and ocean view

middle: view from living room to garden

bottom: terrace

photographer: Rômulo Fialdine

69

ITAPOROROCA HOUSE
ITAPOROROCA•BRAZIL

RICARDO SALEM AND BEATRIZ REGIS BITTENCOURT

Ricardo Salem was chosen to design and build this magnificent home at Itapororoca beach, and given a simple directive: the house had to be, in spirit and form, the face of Brazil. The owner, a long-time resident of Europe, wanted her children, when visiting Trancoso during the holidays, to live in a typical Brazilian dwelling without losing their 'Tupiniquim' roots. After sitting on the original plot for several days, the client and designer began to visualize, little by little, what the home would look like. Itapororoca beach's special feature is that although the houses are right by the sea, they are still surrounded by dense native vegetation, providing them with complete seclusion.

The next step was to build the house while preserving trees as much as possible. Like a flickering slow-motion picture, the images of the house were transferred from the creative mind of Ricardo to the eyes of the client—what the main house, the children's pavilion, the dining room together with the barbecue, and the kitchen, and so on would look like. The idea was to build on the idea of the old communal Indian villages. The articulation is done around the main building, an open living room, situated between the kitchen/dining block and the parents' and guests' block. A large terrace is in fact a reproduction of the old Indian 'ocas'. With a work of interlaced liana, the same kind made by the Yanomamis living in the north of Brazil, the space is magic and, when it is prepared for parties, takes on an ethereal ambience which gives an insight into how the original inhabitants of the land may have lived.

Beatriz transformed the early dream into reality. As time went by, it has become a local icon, known as the 'Ocas' house.

top right: view of house from top of hill

bottom right: detail of wooden roof so characteristic of region

opposite top: site plan

opposite bottom: barbecue, dining room and kitchen

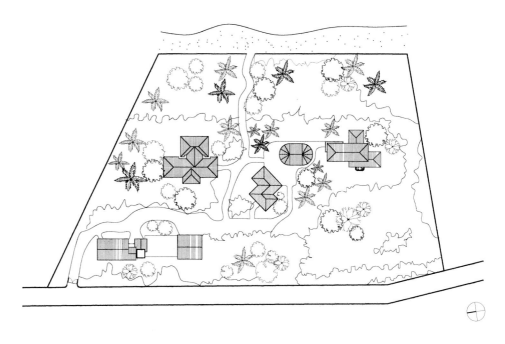

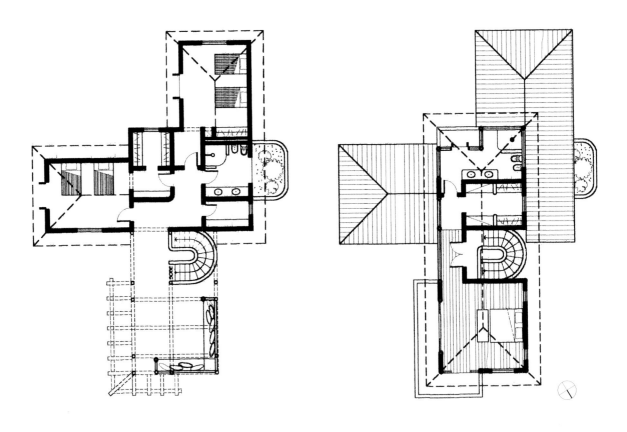

ITAPOROROCA HOUSE

opposite top left: lower level floor plan—main house

opposite top right: upper level floor plan—main house

opposite bottom: north module—main house's veranda

top: south module—children's house; bathroom

above: north module—main house; master bedroom view from veranda
on upper level

left: detail of entrance door—craftwork by local artisans, managed by
Ricardo Salem

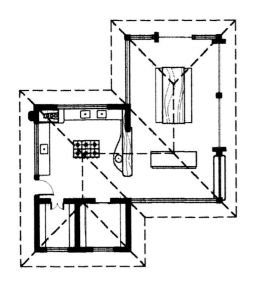

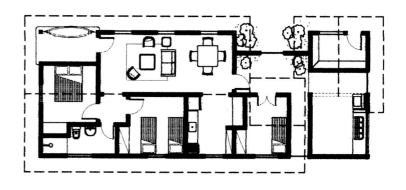

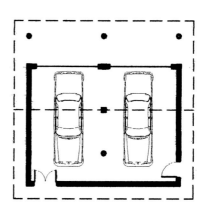

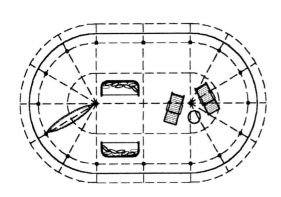

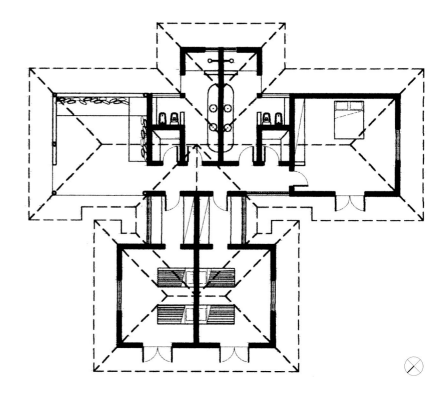

ITAPOROROCA HOUSE

top left: floor plan of barbeque, dining area and kitchen

top right: tenant's house floor plan

middle left: veranda floor plan

middle right: garage floor plan

right: children's house floor plan

opposite top: interior view of barbeque area

opposite bottom left: south module—children's house; veranda

opposite bottom right: interlacing of natural fiber

photographer: Célio Alves Rodrigues Jr

LARANJEIRAS BEACH HOUSE

LARANJEIRAS BEACH•PARATY•RIO DE JANEIRO•BRAZIL

FABRIZIO CECCARELLI

Designing this magnificent residence at Laranjeiras beach, Fabrizio Ceccarelli once again applied the basis of his architecture: the use of natural regional elements in construction, together with some typical urban elements. The house is positioned on land directly facing the ocean, with the rough hillside of Serra do Mar, the mouth of a river, and the perfectly preserved almond trees forming the surroundings.

The residence was built under these almond trees and is perfectly integrated with the vegetation introduced by the landscape designer, Mona Milan. The house comprises two levels in perfect harmony with its surroundings. At the same time, it faces the panoramic view and is protected by its own architectonic composition.

Fabrizio jokes with the colors and the forms. The bedrooms, hidden by the large roof, are linked with balconies that are open to the wide internal spaces. The unwary visitor entering the house is surprised by the bridges and walkways and by different colors that intersect the various rooms—old pink, straw yellow, opaque white, and carbon blue.

The swimming pool forms a dynamic element in the composition of space. Its water 'frames' the living room, the veranda, the deck, and the bedrooms, dressing them with different shades. Its water, fed by fountains, emits a calm and agreeable sound that echoes throughout the complex.

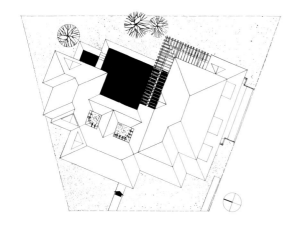

above: site plan

right: view of swimming pool and living room showing bridge, which opens to winter garden

opposite top: master bedroom 'framed' by swimming pool, facing ocean

opposite bottom: main façade facing beach

LARANJEIRAS BEACH HOUSE

opposite: view from terrace to swimming pool

top: sketch

above: circulation over swimming pool

left: view of swimming pool with terrace, living room and fountain

LARANJEIRAS BEACH HOUSE

opposite: view of the living room showing the winter garden

above: view from the balcony facing the beach

top right: living room in front of the swimming pool with natural material furnishings and curtains blocking part of the landscape

photographer: Sérgio Pagano

MARCOS ACAYABA

On a slope of land located 150 meters (492 feet) from the beach and 70 meters high (230 feet) inside the condominium of Tijucopava, this house was erected, with four floors supported by three wood and concrete pillars. The dense native vegetation of the Atlantic Forest on the site has been completely preserved. The triangular geometry of the structure, rigid in its shape, not only allowed the preservation of native plants and trees but also permitted a free rich and dynamic manipulation of internal spaces, which communicate with the external environment.

By crossing a bridge from the street, one enters the property and faces the main body of the house through the kitchen and the living room. A step below is the three-bedroom area with a balcony that overlooks the sea. A step above is a large and open space formed by the roof terrace, with a 2-meter (6.5-foot) cantilevered border for protection against the tropical rains. Standing on the top of this, one can see the ocean and the top of the hill. Hanging between the three sets of diagonal trusses that form the base of the house is the service area, with another bridge leading to the ground.

Continuing in the same style, the relationship between the levels is organic, such as a tree trunk skewering a spiral stairway suspended by steel cables.

The windows are simple and economically made—the central panes of glass are fixed and installed directly in the frame while the side-panes slide gently on narrow tracks carved in the wood. Rainwater is directed to the soil from the roof through five hanging blue tubes—these guarantee natural humidity.

The materials used in the construction are light and practical: triangular plaques, precast in lightweight concrete, for the floors and roof, with parapets and industrialized plywood panels for the walls. These light materials of small dimensions allowed four workers to build the house in just four months.

It can be said that this house represents a synthesis of what Acayaba has studied and sought to achieve in his working life. For him, experiences with different materials allowed the development of new structures and new construction techniques. The way he has developed the structural use of wood has made it easy to handle and adaptable to any type of land. The house's support base of only three points allows minimal interference with the living area and the surrounding landscape.

With this unique and personal house, Acayaba has reminded us of the concepts of Frank Lloyd Wright in which organic forms and the humanization of space are fundamental.

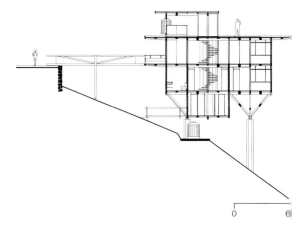

0   6

top right: section
bottom right: northeast view
opposite top: entrance bridge
opposite bottom: west view

82

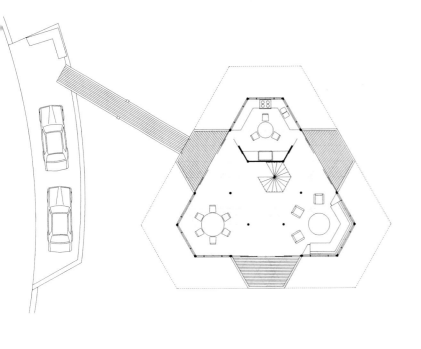

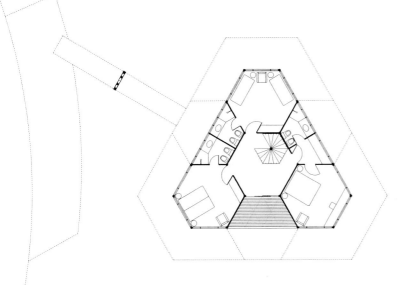

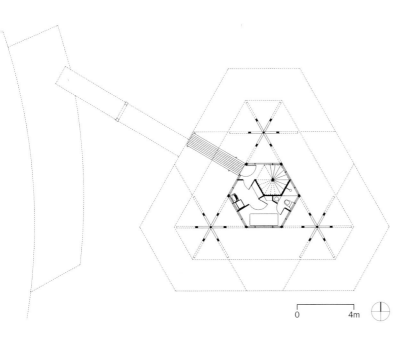

0   4m

MARCOSACAYABA**HOUSE,**TIJUCOPAVA

opposite: view from south

top left: floor plan of kitchen and living area

middle left: floor plan of bedroom area

left: floor plan or service area

top right: kitchen

above: master bedroom

85

MARCOSACAYABA**HOUSE,**TIJUCOPAVA
top: pillars
right: living room
opposite top: living room
opposite bottom: roof terrace
photographer: Nelson Kon

PARAQUEIRA BRASILEIRA

BEBERIBE/URUAÚ LAGOON•CEARÁ•BRAZIL

GERSON CASTELO BRANCO

With wonderful views exploited by Gerson Castelo Branco, this house was designed for a business couple with three children as a weekend meeting place for family and friends. It is located where the ocean meets the dunes and the beautiful wide Uruaú Lagoon.

Taking advantage of the natural declivity of the land, Gerson's project places the viewer in a small private paradise without being monotonous, a fault of many of the old rural houses. The outlook from three levels captures the natural ocean breeze ventilation with no need for air conditioning.

The house is entered through the intermediate level, crossing a suspended ramp over a mirror of water. Openings ensure that the rooms below, including the kitchen, wine cellar, servants' rooms and bathroom, are all naturally ventilated. Also on this level are the swimming pool, sauna, the games room, and a garage for cars and boats. The main entrance goes directly to the living room and the theater room, which are enhanced by three belvederes that open to a beautiful exterior view.

The eucalyptus timber is one of the house's highlights, along with the roof's special timber, *cavaco*, from Pará, a northern state of Brazil, and *ipê*, a Brazilian wood used for the doors and window frames.

The widespread use of glass allows a total integration with the rich local environment. At its highest point, the roof is like a delta wing or hang-glider shape, which is also one of the architect's registered landmarks and an important element of his architecture.

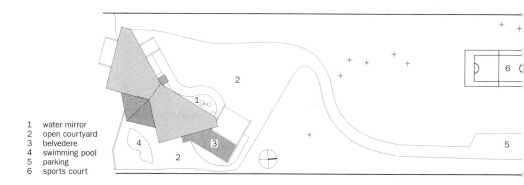

1 water mirror
2 open courtyard
3 belvedere
4 swimming pool
5 parking
6 sports court

right: site plan

opposite: belvedere facing ocean

PARAQUEIRABRASILEIRA

opposite: house view from lagoon

top: house at sunset

above: access façade and mirror of water

left: leisure area

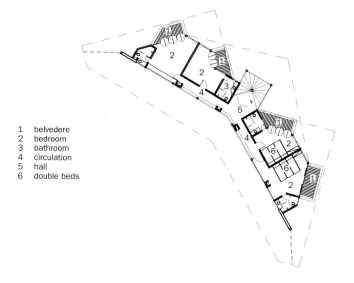

1 belvedere
2 bedroom
3 bathroom
4 circulation
5 hall
6 double beds

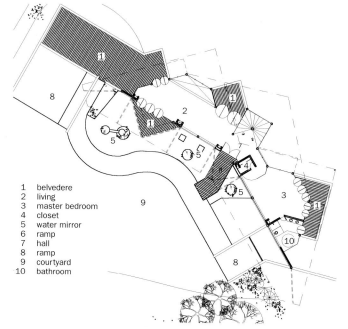

1 belvedere
2 living
3 master bedroom
4 closet
5 water mirror
6 ramp
7 hall
8 ramp
9 courtyard
10 bathroom

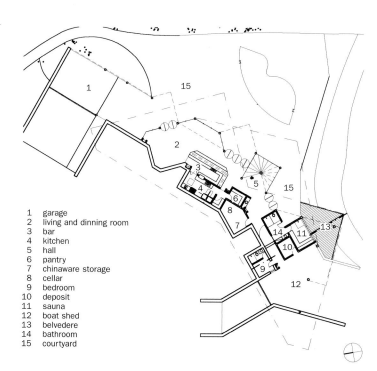

1 garage
2 living and dinning room
3 bar
4 kitchen
5 hall
6 pantry
7 chinaware storage
8 cellar
9 bedroom
10 deposit
11 sauna
12 boat shed
13 belvedere
14 bathroom
15 courtyard

PARAQUEIRA BRASILEIRA

top left: living room (home theater)

middle left: games area

top right: upper level floor plan

middle right: ground level floor plan

bottom right: lower level floor plan

opposite: external living room

92

PARAQUEIRABRASILEIRA

top: main bathroom

middle: guest bedroom

bottom: master bedroom

opposite top: section

opposite bottom: large double-size beds

photographer: Tadeu Lubambo

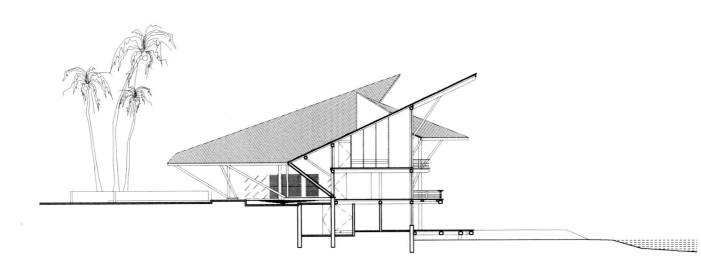

PINGO **D'ÁGUA** HOUSE
PINGO D'ÁGUA BEACH•ILHA GRANDE•ANGRA DOS REIS•RIO DE JANEIRO•BRAZIL

FABRIZIO CECCARELLI

Pingo D'Água Beach is a 600-meter (1970 feet) sweep of private beach on Ilha Grande. Fabrizio Ceccarelli was asked to develop a special house here, while preserving the local flora and fauna. The house is located in a very privileged position, in a natural amphitheater formed by the jungle and the Apa dos Tamoios reserve.

Before beginning the project, Ceccarelli carefully considered a number of different local factors, such as the sea, the rain, the winds, the jungle, and the region's strong Indian tradition. Relying heavily on the Indian tradition, he designed a new concept of space and open-air living.

The central pavilion is thought of as being a large Indian 'oca' (the home of the old Indians) that shelters the communal areas, and is defined with symbolic and composed elements. The swimming pool enters the living area, there is a bridge to the dining space, and a small stream defines the conversation area and the veranda. The resting area, a games room, is the only closed space and is situated on a kind of mezzanine level. The central idea was to revive the Indians' ancient way of living where all activity occurred in a large, wide central room.

This distribution of interlaced rooms throughout the complex forms a large 'necklace' around the swimming pool and the living spaces are protected by the wonderful integration of the surrounding jungle landscape, developed by architect Louis Marcelo Codeiro Nunes.

To better achieve a symbiosis with nature and the environment, traditional materials are widely used: wood from a swamp, organic floors, vegetation roofs, and sisal wraps.

Taking the project as a whole, we can see that the swimming pool serves as a catalyzing element with its sounds, reflections, and colors entering the communal, private, and service areas.

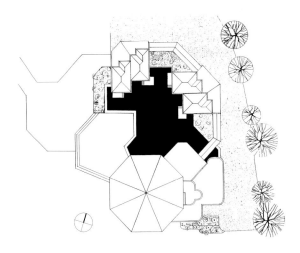

above: site plan

right: aerial view of beach

opposite top: main façade from beach

opposite bottom: central pavilion and bedrooms

PINGO **D'ÁGUA** HOUSE
opposite top: sketch
opposite bottom: bridge to dining area
above: swimming pool and view from bedrooms

99

PINGO **D'ÁGUA** HOUSE

above: swimming pool, solarium, and view from bedrooms

top right: detail of roof structure

opposite: internal view of living area

photographer: Sérgio Pagano

SÃO SEBASTIÃO BEACH HOUSE

SÃO SEBASTIÃO•SÃO PAULO•BRAZIL

BOTTI RUBIN

With sensitivity, rationalism, and total integration with the surroundings, this house was built by Marc Rubin—the renowned architect and founder of Botti Rubin Architects partnership. The house is located on the São Sebastião coastline, 200km (124 miles) north of São Paulo, Brazil, and was built for a family who loves sailing and being in touch with nature.

This house was designed using structure as a strong architectural argument, sometimes bordering on high-tech, which has been a Botti Rubin trademark in their search for quality contemporary architecture.

However, this house is not high-tech and blends perfectly into its natural surroundings—a steep stony hillside that slopes down to a rocky shore in calm waters.

The project evolved during construction in order to conform to the real contorted pattern of the grounds, including hidden rocks, which no earlier survey was able to spot precisely, and the trees of the typical tropical forest found on this site.

The house was built using natural materials: stone retaining walls and wooden structures for the roofs (the overhangs of which provide shade and protection from occasional heavy rain). Large panes of glass and brickwork enclose the living quarters at various levels, from the parking access down to the bedrooms, then down to the living room, and then further to the swimming pool, barbeque area and the boat landing deck at sea level.

This house is a classic Botti Rubin in its quality contemporary architecture.

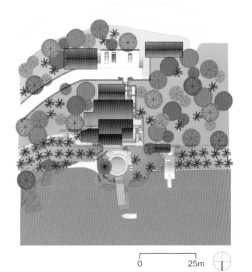

0   25m

parking level

bedrooms level

entrance level

living room level

swimming pool level

above: site plan

top right: view from sea

right: section

opposite: view from swimming pool area

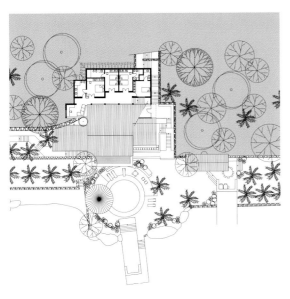

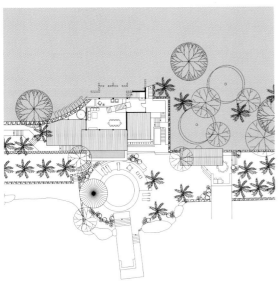

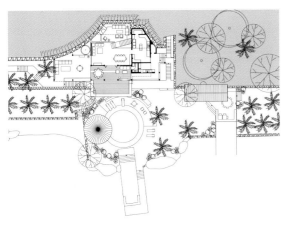

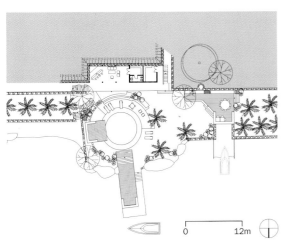

0   12m

SÃO **SEBASTIÃO** BEACH **HOUSE**

opposite: living room

top left: site plan—bedroom level

middle left: site plan—entrance level

bottom left: site plan—living level

left: site plan—sea and swimming pool level

above: terraces

photographer: Gerson Bilezikjian

105

SÍTIO **CARABABA** NORTH **COAST**

ALAGOAS COAST•ALAGOAS•BRAZIL

HUMBERTA FARIAS

Sítio Carababa is located in the beautiful landscape of the north coast of Alagoas, which is a favored place for weekend and summer holiday beach houses.

The major challenge facing the architect was to design a house where nature and the spectacular view would combine to give the house an identity, without losing its character in the imposing landscape.

As Humberta says: "The source of inspiration was the house's surroundings—the insinuated elegance of the swamp's roots which jump from the earth. From that, we designed the roof's edge, which features fluctuating balconies and the roof's movement supported by wood columns built 'free' from the house's structure. This design bears a strong similarity to the native fishing *palafitta* houses."

The use of wood can be seen in many aspects of the building's construction: in the straight lines of the façade, in the structural beams, in the parapet of the balconies, in the doors and windows made of wood and tempered glass, and in the stair that links the dining room to the mezzanine.

The wide use of materials such as stone, timber, and tiles make the residence–region relationship a harmonious one.

Taking advantage of the land's natural inclination, the house has three floors. The distribution of rooms respects magnetic orientation and places significance on thermal comfort, which is very important in this northeastern area. As a consequence, the house has a wide and high ambience and a particular effort was made to capture the dominant winds passing through. One of the owner's, a very skilful sailor, has used a special treatment to protect the wood and other materials from the effects of the sea.

The owners were very clear about their needs, and not only accepted the architectural proposal but also participated in the construction process. This made the work easier and faster. In the end, after the successful completion of this residence, they decided to move permanently into this beautiful house, not far from Maceió, the Alagoas capital. From one side, you can see the swamps and roots and from the other the coconut trees; straight ahead is the horizon. Observing the house from outside, it is perfectly integrated and becomes a part of the landscape to be contemplated.

top right: posterior façade

right: site plan

opposite: lateral façade and bedroom balconies

0   10m

SÍTIO **CARABABA** NORTH **COAST**

opposite top: north façade

opposite bottom: house by night

top left: brise detail and wood parapet

above: lateral view from terrace, mezzanine and dining
balcony

left: bedroom balconies

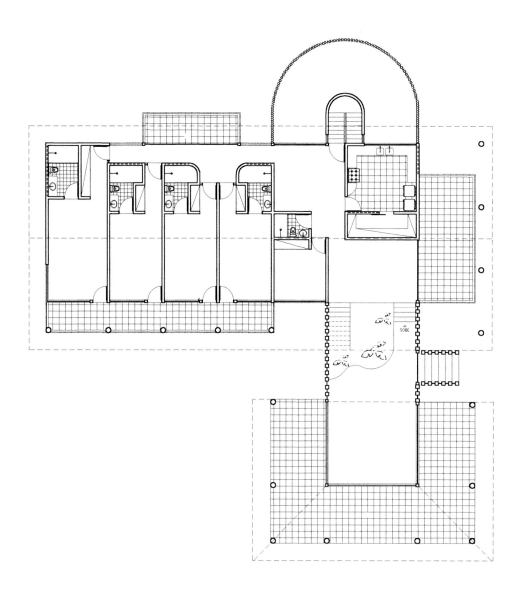

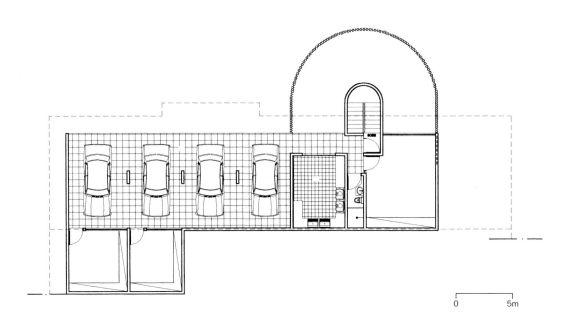

SÍTIO **CARABABA** NORTH **COAST**

top: upper level floor plan

above: garage level floor plan

opposite top: view of living and mezzanine

opposite bottom: dining balcony

photographer: Cacá Bratke

110

SÍTIO **NATURA** (TREE HOUSE)

SÍTIO NATURA/NOVA VIÇOSA•BAHIA•BRAZIL

FRANZ KRAJCBERG

There are a number of theories about the origin of the very first house, about the need for humans to leave the caves behind but protect themselves against the harshness of nature. We have always required shelter from storms, wild animals, and even other people. When one studies very early architecture, it becomes clear that most structures were built in open areas and focused on religion—monuments to the glory of the gods and the extraordinary capacity of the human mind. When humans sought to shelter themselves in closed dwellings within four walls, they naturally made their homes sympathetic to the primitive environment and often crafted these dwellings from natural timber.

This is what we see in Franz Krajcberg's wonderful Tree House in Bahia. From a 2.6-meter-diameter (8.5 feet) 'branch' received from a friend, he conceived what was to become his refuge, home, and shelter.

Built 25 years ago, the house has adjusted well during the passage of time, and the many different objects collected by Krajcberg in all those years of travel and hard work. Four years ago, the sculptor was taken by surprise when he noticed that one of the beams was full of termites, clearly a serious problem for the structure's integrity. The task of getting rid of the termites, preserving the existing beam, and reinforcing it was, in his words, much more difficult than the actual construction of the house.

In this house, nature, the environment, and people are in complete harmony in the simplicity of a living room, bedroom, and terrace, facing the ocean through the treetops. This is enough to shelter Krajcberg and provide, in a very romantic and magical way, that simple thing that the rest of us call 'home.'

right: Franz Krajcberg holding fantastic artwork sculpted from burnt and dead wood

opposite: night view of house; circular stairway in background

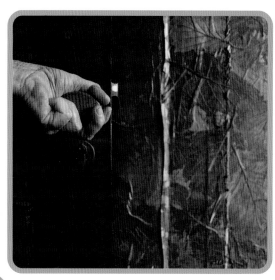

SÍTIO **NATURA** (TREE HOUSE)

opposite top: bedroom ambience
opposite bottom: entrance door and living/kitchen
above: wooden door opened against recovered wall in
bedroom with old, dry leaves and branches
left: bedroom ambience
photographer: Márcio Scavone

115

TOQUINHO HOUSE
PRAIA DO TOQUINHO/IPOJUCA•PERNAMBUCO•BRAZIL

BORSOI & ASSOCIATES

This house covers 876 square meters (9430 square feet), developed as "several spaces inside one lonely space," according to the Argentinean architect Roberto Ghione. It stands on land comprising 8000 square meters (86,112 square feet) facing Recife's ocean. Borsoi designed his summer house together with Janete Ferreira da Costa and Roberta Gil Borsoi. With his deep knowledge of modern architectonic thematics, Borsoi plays with different heights and scales where the simple geometric elements, such as cubes, rectangles, and circles, form an integrated, contemporary space. Da Costa and Gil Borsoi, with sensitivity and sophistication, enhance the space with important Brazilian furniture, art, and crafts. The house was designed with two large inclined roofs covered with nailed blue ceramics. Large doors and glass openings expose the house to the exceptional local environment. The interior and exterior reflect each other.

Inside, the open living/dining/garden space allows a sense of 'free' life without any borders or limits. Outside, similarly, the magisterial landscape, constructed by Ofra Grinfeder, runs freely to the beach and the ocean without any fences or barriers to restrain it. What one sees before anything else is the deep respect for the theme of 'architecture.' The work transcends regionalism to become one of the pillars of contemporary South American leisure architecture. Borsoi's work is grounded in Brazilian modernism, complemented by contemporary finishings such as the floor's acrylic cover, which contrasts with the white ceramic tile from Brennand, and the inox steel beams and columns of the terrace that highlight the lighting and transparency of the work. The interior architecture, designed by Janete Ferreira da Costa and Roberta Gil Borsoi, is full of the characteristic elements of Brazilian arts. Whether canvas, sculptures, or objects, they each enrich and complement Borsoi's vision.

Parodiando (from parody), an old Tibetan proverb, says "where there is veneration, everything emits light." This is what can be seen in this simple but sophisticated house, where the first impression is crucial. It engraves its images forever.

top right: side view of house
bottom right: guest house
opposite top: daytime view of house
opposite bottom: night view of house

TOQUINHO HOUSE
opposite top: frontal view of guest house
opposite bottom: swimming pool, garden, and ocean
left: view from garden and guest house lake with lighting designed by Borsoi
middle: frontal view of main house
bottom: main entrance 'corridor'

opposite top: night view from garden and side façade
opposite middle: guest house by night
opposite bottom: vibrant colors of floors close to main entrance
above: entrance door with stairway to left

TOQUINHO HOUSE

above: internal ambience on two levels

right: view of internal garden through to ground level and upper hall

opposite top: lighting on open windows facing ocean brings outside in

opposite bottom left: view from upper level to ground level focusing on stairway and large glass opening in façade

opposite bottom right: internal ambience living with floor detail—white resin floor cover and white ceramic Brennand tile

photographer: Tadeu Lubambo

CHILE

CHILE

Chile's coast has more than 4000 kilometers (2485 miles) of beaches on the Pacific Ocean. In the north, golden sandy beaches with clear, calm waters are ideal for sport and fishing. In the center, there are places where the blue–green ocean blends harmoniously with the vegetation. Along the entire coast, Chile's famous seafood is rich in variety and taste.

Tongoy is situated 430 kilometers (267 miles) from the capital Santiago and is surrounded by the 'Lengua de Vaca' mountains—where the Andes meet the Costa mountains. The Playa Grande is found south of Tongoy and the Praia dos Socos some 14 kilometers (9 miles) further on.

In the mid 19th century, when Chile was the world's largest copper supplier, Tongoy thrived as the home to a vast copper smelting works. When this era came to an end, the city was reinvented as a resort and also grew into a prosperous fishing area. Tongoy is now an ideal place to have a holiday home.

Zapallar, located on Chile's central coast, is 180 kilometers (112 miles) north of Santiago. A small and sheltered bay, surrounded by hills protects Zapallar from strong coastal winds. The local area, originally a farm, was created as a summer holiday place by the previous owner who decided, after visiting Nice and Cannes in 1851, to donate land to his friends on the condition that they built their houses within two years.

This peculiar origin has saved the area from the kind of predatory tourism that exists nowadays. People were concerned about the land, the roads, and the environment. They not only built houses, but also constructed charming streets, ramps to the edge of the ocean, and cultivated a small forest.

Perhaps the most important architectural feature was that Le Courbusier's famous house 'Maison Errazuriz' was built in Zapallar. Unfortunately, it no longer exists.

KLOTZ HOUSE

PLAYA GRANDE • TONGOY • CHILE

MATHIAS KLOTZ GERMAIN

For a land area of 5700 square meters (61,355 square feet), Klotz Germain designed and built a 99-square-meter (1065 square feet) summerhouse. It is a rectangular house raised 30 centimeters (12 inches) up from the earth.

At first sight, the house appears as a blind façade with a curved bridge forming the main entrance to the house. In reality, the façade walls face the sun and have large openings allowing in the sun and natural light.

Two galleries comprise the site plan. On the ground floor, a 2-meter (6.5-foot) gallery consists of the entrance, the stairs, the bathrooms and a small bedroom. A second 4-meter (13-foot) gallery contains the master bedroom, the kitchen/dining room, and a high-ceilinged living room. On the first floor, the bedrooms are far away from the façade and facing the sea, allowing space for two terraces. The stairway and the corridor to the bedrooms continue the gallery concept.

The woodwork, the white interior, the openings in the walls, the added and subtracted elements, the proportions, and the articulated horizontal lines of the wood façade all blend to create a work on a human scale in contrast to the vast surrounding landscape.

The Klotz House appears almost as a transitory object. That is why it is raised 30 centimeters (12 inches) from the earth to create a fragile and uncertain materiality.

As a summerhouse, the Klotz House was envisaged to be a retreat rather than a stable home. The furniture and facilities are nothing more than basic. The structure and finishes are made of plain pinewood, augmenting the house's transitory, camp-like character.

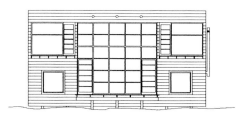

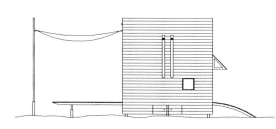

KLOTZ HOUSE

top right: east façade; entrance ramp

middle right: west elevation

bottom right: south elevation

opposite top: night view of house

opposite bottom: west façade

127

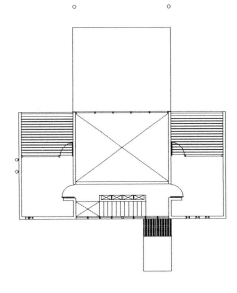

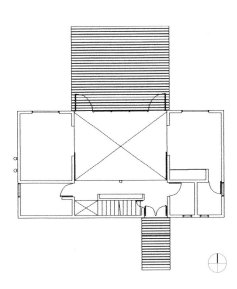

KLOTZ HOUSE

opposite: double-height living room
top left: upper level
middle left: lower level
above: double-height living room
left: upper level terrace
photographer: Juan Purcell

ZAPALLAR HOUSE I
ZAPALLAR•CHILE

ENRIQUE BROWNE & ASSOCIATES

This project is a summer home on the Pacific coast for a couple without children. The house occupies an area of land that sits in front of a two-story house. It was a condition of the sale of the lot that the new house should not obstruct sea views from the pre-existing house.

It was decided that the new residence would be built into the edge of a rocky cliff that reaches to the ocean. In this way, the roof is a continuation of the garden-terrace above. The house occupies the whole front of the terrain, with spectacular views of the sea. One descends to the house by a stairway that overlooks an English patio and water collector. The service areas abut the interior side, freeing the western edge for living spaces such as the living room and bedrooms.

The house has many flexible uses—the two sofa beds in the living room can be separated by curtains to accommodate guests, and the second bedroom also serves as accommodation or as an office for the home's owner. The living room and bedrooms overlook a terrace with a lawn, partially covered by a horizontal blind of bamboo-like slats that provide protection from the western sun. This blind goes around the upper axis to protect the house when it is not occupied. From the terrace, one can descend to a pool formed on the rocks or directly toward the sea.

The double helix of pillars, which virtually delimits the upper and lower terraces, is made of hammered concrete in order to give a stony aspect. On the stairs, the pool, other external elements, and stones from the site were used to mimic the house as part of the immediate scenery.

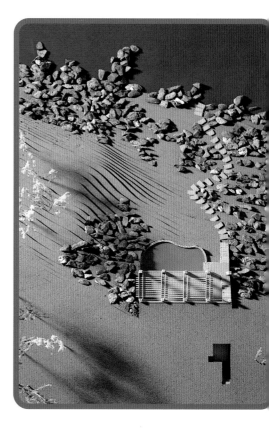

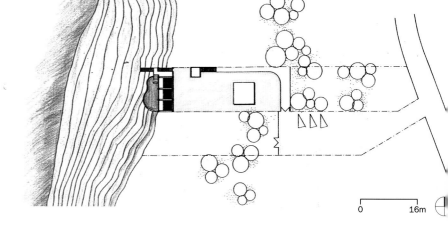

top right: aerial view of house
right: site plan
opposite top: floor plan
opposite bottom: view from sea
photographers: Guy Wenborne and Enrique Browne

0   16m

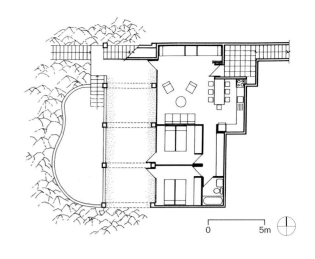

ZAPALLAR HOUSE II
ZAPALLAR•CHILE

ENRIQUE BROWNE & ASSOCIATES

The land on which this summerhouse is built is long, narrow, and quite steep. The property runs from north to south along Highway F-30 on its upper boundary and along Carrera Pinto Street on its lower boundary. It has splendid views of the beach and the bay. The wooded terrain presented two problems: one, the terrain ran to the south received very little sun (although Chile is in the southern hemisphere) and two, regulations dictated that construction should have a set-back line of 7.5 meters (25 feet) parallel to the ground. These conditions meant that the house must be at its highest point as close as possible to the highway, as well as breaking the program into distinct volumes so as to adapt to the set-back lines and to maximize sunshine and views.

Toward the highway, the house is enclosed by a stone wall and translucent thermo panes for receiving sunlight from the north. Illuminated at night, it resembles a huge horizontal lamp. Toward the south, the house opens explosively, rotating and offering different aspects according to the viewer's

movement. In fact, the house has at least six façades. Furthermore, depending on one's point of view, the house appears to hover above the earth, or as part of the wooded landscape, given its outer coating of oxidized copper.

There are different interior and exterior ramps and stairs, offering various circulations. The flagstone of these circulations helps to contain the thrust of the terrain.

The program was divided into three superimposed 'boats' or 'leaves' rotated among themselves to adapt to the set-back lines and to obtain different views of the distant scenery. The 'boats' are connected by glass-covered ramps that feature a zigzagging circulation that looks out toward the town or the beach.

The master bedroom is on the upper level. The living-dining-kitchen area is located on the intermediate level. The children's rooms are on the lowest level. For privacy, the guestroom is located at the far end of the house. As a whole, the layout suggests a branch with leaves.

Under the 'boats' or 'leaves,' a large swimming pool crosses the house. Inside, most furniture is built-in. Two lighting fixtures were specially designed. One lights the curve of the road and the other the height of the stairs. The blue light of the latter gives an aqueous appearance to the 'boats.'

right: north façade from west by night
opposite top: view from east of circulation volume
opposite middle left: view from south
opposite middle right: view from west during construction
opposite bottom: pool and bay

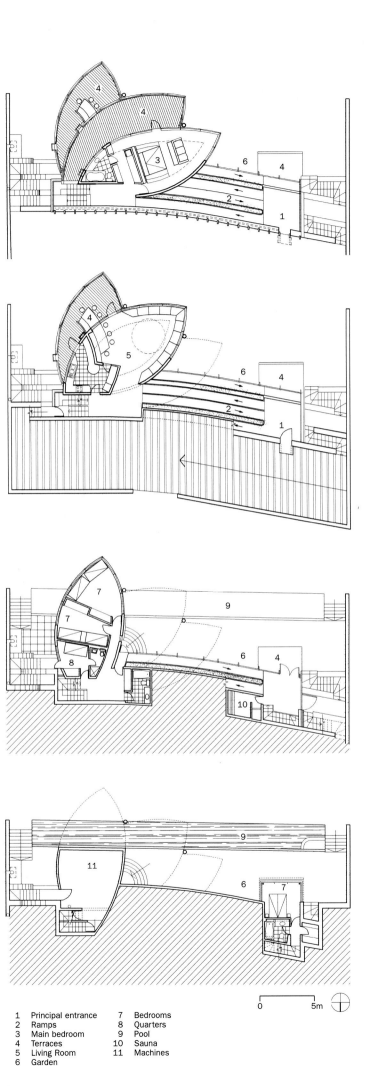

1	Principal entrance	7	Bedrooms
2	Ramps	8	Quarters
3	Main bedroom	9	Pool
4	Terraces	10	Sauna
5	Living Room	11	Machines
6	Garden		

0   5m

ZAPALLAR HOUSE II

opposite top left: father's bedroom

opposite middle left: living-dining room

opposite middle right: view from hall

opposite bottom right: living area

top left: upper level

middle top left: intermediate level

middle bottom left: lower level

bottom left: lowest level

top right: view of ramps

photographers: Guy Wenborne and Enrique Browne

PERU

PERU

Lima, the main entrance to Peru, sits on the edge of the Pacific Ocean. It is a mixed city with pre-Hispanic, colonial, and modern elements, and it is surrounded by nature: the ocean, desert, islands, mountains, and vegetation. In the historic downtown, there are delightful colonial churches and houses; further south, there is a huge preserved natural environment, 'Pantanos da Villa,' a safe shelter for more than 150 different kind of birds and the archeological site of Pachacamac. To the north is the National Reserve of Lachay, a natural habitat for fauna and flora, and there are archeological sites from prehistoric cultures in Paramonga.

North or south, many summer towns and beaches are surrounded by dramatic views of the Pacific Ocean. Driving south along the Panamericana Highway, bordering the Pacific, there are many beautiful beaches—idyllic spots for a relaxing weekend. This is where Playa Bonita and Playa Palillos are located. One of the main characteristics of Peruvian beaches is their wild landscape. Some are perched on the edge of large prairies, others beneath cliffs or hills. The ocean's deep green color is due to the richness of its plankton. The beaches possess a wide emotional scale—from still and sparkling to gothically wild and stormy.

MORI HOUSE IN PLAYA BONITA

PLAYA BONITA • LIMA • PERU

ALEXIA LÉON ANGELL

This house, built on one of the four squares of land measuring 12.5 square meters (134.5 square feet) in the main quadrangular settlement of Playa Bonita, commands attention with its capacity to be a conventional summerhouse in a very small space. In the middle of a large and wild landscape, it creates an intimate space for the owner without compromising the desert's intrinsic nature: its emptiness.

Three blocks define the house: two parallel blocks—a community one facing north and a residential one facing south—and a transverse services block. A courtyard links the blocks. It attracts and disperses the light diagonally in its interior and protects the space from wind.

This courtyard aligns the functions of the house both horizontally—the living/dining, residential, and services area—and vertically links the upper level through a stairway path (a vertical incision of transparent crystal) that passes over the house's entrance and goes up to the terrace, which faces the far ocean. This ascending motion has its completion in the reflected light of a crystal fence located in the center. Controlling this movement is a vertical element that supports, on two levels, a laundry and barbecue. Low-cost materials were used and were integral in taking advantage of the Peruvian coastal climate and the house's logical design.

This house also draws attention by achieving the perfect balance between the house's spaces and the richness of its relations. It has earned the architect the honor of being one of the six finalists for the second Mies Van Der Rohe Prize for Latin American architects.

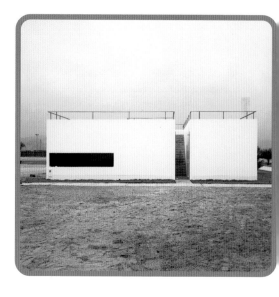

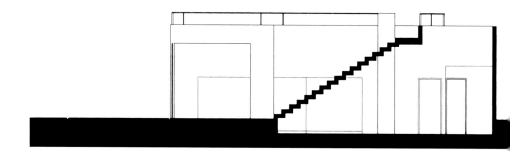

top right: entrance to house

right: section

opposite: south and north façade

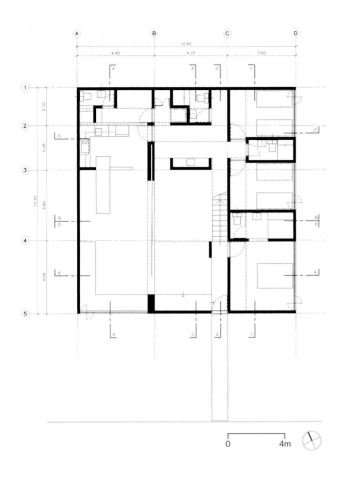

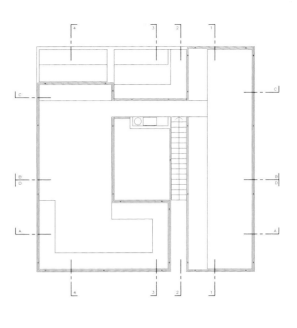

MORI HOUSE IN PLAYA BONITA

opposite: view of courtyard

top left: lower level

top right: upper level

middle left: stair

left: internal view of dining and living area

above: stair

photographer: Juan Enrique Bedoya

PALILLOS HOUSE
PLAYA PALILLOS • LIMA • PERU

EMILIO SOYER NASH

The Peruvian coast is unusual because it has been formed by some of the drier deserts on earth although it lies next to the ocean. These features can clearly be seen in the two beautiful houses built by Emilio Soyer Nash. Both are built on a rocky, sandy slope with a steep incline toward the ocean. This necessitated the construction of container walls, columns, and reinforced concrete beams.

Both houses have the same 'mirror' plan, although one is lower than the other. The sole variations between the two are the stairs and the floor surfaces. The main entrance is on the upper level through the parking area, with an entrance to the master bedroom or to the semi-covered balcony through a stairway in the intermediate level. To one side, on the same level, is the kitchen and, on the other, the living room. Beyond the terrace lies a courtyard containing a lush display of vegetation at its center. At the end of the courtyard, there is a small swimming pool looking out to the breathtaking view of the Peruvian coast. More stairs reach the lower level, which houses the remaining bedrooms.

The house is painted in white both inside and out and this makes a beautiful contrast to the blue sky and its arid landscape surrounds.

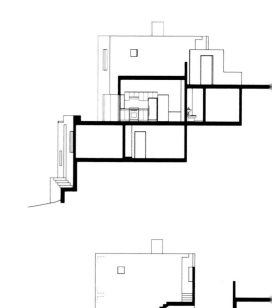

top and middle right: longitudinal sections
right: side view of two blocks
opposite top: front view of two blocks
opposite bottom: view of stone walls

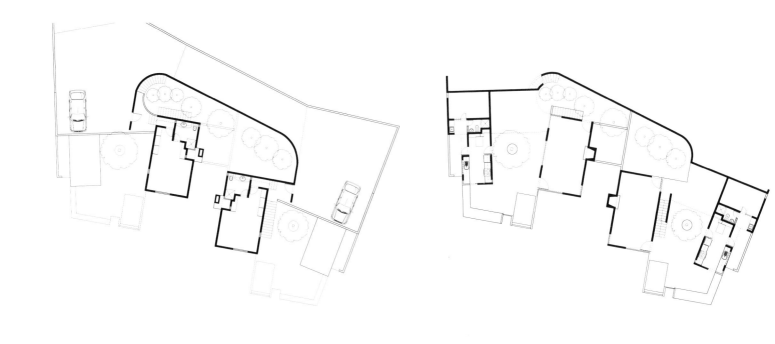

144

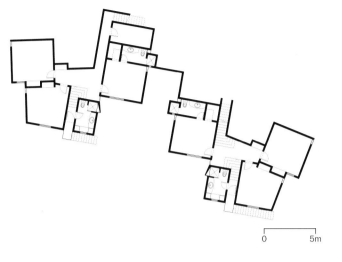

PALILLOS HOUSE

opposite top left: entrance level site plan
opposite top right: intermediate level site plan
opposite bottom: view of middle courtyard
top left: bedrooms level
above: parking entrance
left: courtyard view of middle level
photographer: Emilio Soyer Nash

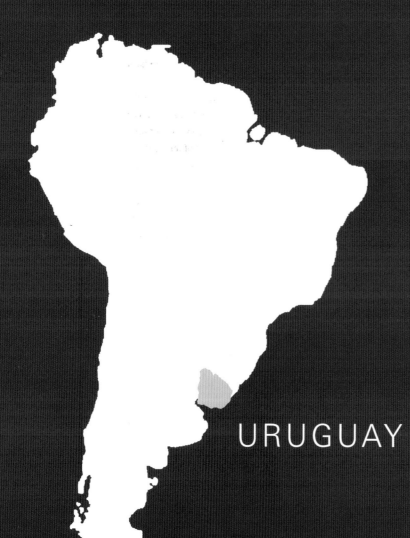

URUGUAY

URUGUAY

At the beginning of the 19th century, Punta del Este was a semi-deserted region visited only by fishermen and sailors. Originally, it was an Indian colony, later becoming a popular fishing area. By 1940, its international fame as a glamorous city below the Ecuador line had begun.

Geographically, it is situated in the southeast of Uruguay, 140 kilometers (87 miles) from the capital, Montevideo. The peninsula lies between the Plata River and the Atlantic Ocean. Affectionately known as 'Punta,' the city was built on sand dunes, which moved daily in accordance with the wind direction, and the realization dawned that planting plenty of vegetation was necessary in order to 'secure' the dunes. This area became the neighborhood called 'ciudad jardín.' On the opposite side of the great peninsula are two islands—Gorriti Island and Wolves Island—which are inhabited by some of the world's biggest sea lions.

The city's strict zoning laws will only permit the construction of high buildings within a certain zone and all other buildings are allowed a maximum of four levels.

Punta has a reputation for being a top tourist destination—not just because of its beautiful scenery but also its welcoming people and fabulous food.

CASA DE PIEDRA
PIEDRA • PUNTA DEL ESTE • URUGUAY

DIEGO FELIX SAN MARTIN—LONNE

'Stone House' is the result of the restoration and enlargement of a cement and stone house, which originally hosted a restaurant managed by the well-known Argentinean gourmand and designer, Mercedes Bosch. More recently, it has been converted into a family house. Its outstanding characteristic is the use of the original materials—stone and naked brick—that mark the house as an icon in the Punta Piedra region. The great challenge for the architects was to design a new project, one which met the client's need for a lighter and cozier visual appearance, but didn't detract from the original character. The solution was to replace brick with the region's *lapacho* wood, which develops a gray tone over time to match the yellowed ochre of the stone.

The original construction was located on a particular area of the Atlantic coast—next to the highway that links the surrounding towns, and where the beach curves onto the rocks—exposing the local houses to the lapping of the ocean at high tide. This meant the house was flooded two or three times a year, depending on storm activity.

The best way to avoid floods was to elevate the ground floor and remove the existing reinforced concrete layer.

The construction had, before the remodeling, the charm of an old ruin, and this was sustained by the restoration, which joined the 'poetic' part of the ruin to the rest of the construction using natural *lapacho* wood. There is an intrinsic dialog between the external stones and the internal wood that was bought from an old warehouse in Montevideo port.

There isn't any symmetry, says architect San Martín, but rather a beach parallel axis, where ruins and new volumes are combined, where the ocean and the beach are the landscape enhancing the expanded interior.

The triangular shape of the land has been followed in the restoration. The new area (formerly the bedrooms) is connected to the main part of the house. The reception area and main entrance, the master bedroom and the music room, are linked through an internal corridor with open windows to the kitchen and the dining room.

The change in materials created a new modulation in the façades, which have turned their outlook to the interesting surroundings and allowed a view from Punta to many parts of the house.

As well as meeting the client's requirements, the architects have captured the surrounding environment, invoking in both the interior and exterior the sensations evoked by wild natural surroundings.

top left: front façade viewed from beach
bottom left: living room deck
opposite top: drawing of façade
opposite bottom: façade perspective

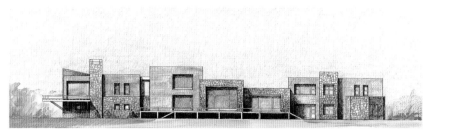

1 master bedroom hall
2 master bedroom corridor
3 closet
4 bathroom
5 master bedroom
6 terrace deck
7 music room
8 storage
9 corridor to bedrooms
10 children's bedrooms
11 children's bathroom
12 service hall
13 service bedroom
14 service bathroom

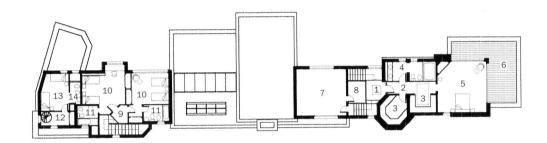

1 main access
2 children's access
3 service access
4 tenant's access
5 entrance hall
6 toilet
7 garage
8 storage
9 living room
10 deck terrace
11 fireplace
12 dining room
13 children's circulation
14 kitchen
15 children's living room
16 children's bedroom
17 children's bathroom
18 bathroom
19 tenant's living room/kitchen
20 tenant's bedroom
21 barbecue

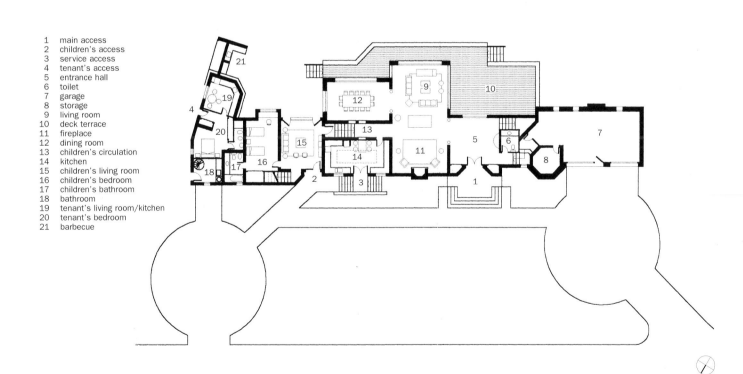

CASA DE PIEDRA

opposite: view from deck facing Punta Del Este

top left: living room circulation to children's area

photographer: Alejandro Leveratto

top middle: view of dining room to living room and deck

top right: view of living room to main hall

middle: upper level

above: ground level

photographer: Daniela MacAdden

FEATURED
ARCHITECTS

BIOGRAPHIES

ALEXIA LÉON ANGELL

Alexia Léon Angell is a young architect who received international acclaim for her first work, 'House in Playa Bonita.' This project was completed in 1998, the same year she was a finalist in the first Iberoamerican Biennial of Architecture, Madrid, Spain. In 2001, she was chosen, among other designers, to participate in the second Mies Van Der Rohe Prize for Latin American Architecture. Between 1993 and 1995, she assisted the architect and professor Juvenal Baracco at the Faculty of Architecture in Lima. In 1996, she formed her own studio and since then has been designing her own projects.

ANNE MARIE SUMNER

Anne Marie Sumner was born in São Paulo and studied architecture at the Faculty of Architecture and Urbanism, at the University of São Paulo. She has a Masters in Philosophy, Human Science and Letters and a Doctorate from the University of São Paulo. Since 1984, she has run her own office—Anne Marie Sumner Arquitetura.

From 1978 to 1993, Anne Marie taught history and theory at the Faculty of Architecture at the Catholic University of Campinas, and since 1990, she has taught at the Department of Projects at the Faculty of Architecture and Urbanism at Mackenzie University in São Paulo.

In 1985 she collaborated with Peter Eisemann and in 1990 she was curator for a major exhibition of his work in the Museum of Modern Art in São Paulo. Since then, she has been linked with Jacques Derrida's deconstruction theories, and has moved her architecture into a natural realm of implantation and framing with the landscape.

Her most important works include: Rodrigo Etchenique Residence, São Paulo (1984); Oswald de Andrade School (in collaboration with the architect Luís Espallargas), São Paulo (1989); Renault Pavillion in Buenos Aires, Argentina (award winner) (1992); Lighting design for the city of São Paulo (1995); Praia do Felix Residence, São Paulo (1998); Theater of the Itaú Cultural Institute, São Paulo (1999).

BORSOI & ASSOCIATES

Acácio Gil Borsoi was born in Rio de Janeiro in 1924 and studied at the Faculty of Architecture at the University of Brazil in Rio. In 1951, he moved to Recife, Pernambuco's capital, accepting an invitation to become a professor at the School of Belles Arts. He was one of the most important 'mentors' in creating a 'Pernambuco style' of architecture and he has been responsible for guiding a generation of architects, both locally and nationally.

He was Professor of Architecture Composition at the Faculty of Architecture, at the Federal University of Pernambuco from 1959 to 1978, and Director of the Engineering and Social Service Division against the Mocambo from 1963 to 1964. This was an important movement in Recife, which helped local people to build practical, low-cost housing through the use of new architectural techniques but traditional building materials.

Borsoi then established Borsoi Associated Architects S/C in Recife. There, he has developed a wide-ranging practice, with many of his works published in magazines and books, and has projects in all fields of public and private architecture.

BOTTI RUBIN

Breaking away from his family's technical tradition, Marc Rubin decided to become an architect when he was introduced to modern Brazilian architecture in Brazil in the late 50s. Studying at Mackenzie University of Architecture—which at that time had a very strong and classical orientation—he and other students rebelled in order to improve the lessons to include discussions on the architecture of Sullivan, Frank Lloyd Wright, and Le Courbusier. At that time, Niemeyer was a national hero, Bauhaus was a discovery, and Neutra, Breuer, and Mis were truly important in the USA and the Lever House of SOM.

Rubin became proficient in Chinese ink water coloring on stretched canson paper, and is familiar with the traditional drawing board and the study of the Classics. This direction made him agile in terms of conception, a characteristic that would be reflected in his future professional life.

In his third year at college, Rubin became a trainee at the Rino Levi Architecture Studio. Rino was a prominent architect in São Paulo City. This experience would later prove to have been vital to his career. When competing in a contest together, Rubin and Alberto Botti decided to establish a partnership. This long-lasting association is no doubt underscored by the differences in the prinicipals' characters and interests—

Botti is more active in urban planning and politics, while Rubin is more concerned with harmonizing ingenious intuition with conceptual and creative reasoning.

CLÁUDIO BERNARDES AND PAULO JACOBSEN

We begin by noting with great sadness the recent passing of Cláudio Bernardes. He was born in Rio de Janeiro and practised the profession of architecture as a culturally sensitive and sanguine responsibility. An architect's son, for 26 years he worked with his friend Paulo Jacobsen, a photographer and architect. Together they managed simultaneously from 30 to 50 projects inside Brazil and they worked on almost 1000 designs in total. Fortunately, their work continues under new management—Jacobsen, Bernardes' son Thiago Bernardes, the third generation of architects in the family, together with a third partner, Miguel Guimarães under the office of Bernardes, Jacobsen, Guimarães Architects.

Their own words best express the philosophy that guides them: "Architecture is an art that develops in the context and culture of a society but also recycles culture, improving during the years without losing the capacity to remain open to influence. This is perhaps the best definition of our work—eyes always wide open to what happens in the world but with a firm link to the arts and culture of Brazil. During these long years together, we have produced several houses in wood and straw, exploring material textures and natural colors."

DAVID BASTOS

Living and working in Salvador, one of Brazil's most beautiful cities, David Fernandes Guimarães Bastos completed his architecture studies in 1981 at the Federal University of Bahia. Along with architecture and design work, David also travels around Brazil lecturing on his professional experiences. His projects are often published in overseas magazines and his architectural work reaches beyond Brazil into places like Portugal and Miami. His different styles of work range from public urban planning projects to residential houses. The inherent baroque spirit of Salvador's city (where there are more than 1000 baroque churches from colonial times), has strongly influenced his work—and it also creates a demand for a sympathetic style. These days, he says he hasn't a definitive style, and open-mindedly approaches the best way to treat a space. He prefers freedom.

Bastos is largely responsible for the revitalization of the docks of Salvador—in 1995, he established his magnificent office in an old warehouse in this area. Following his example, a famous restaurant opened its doors in the same area and later followed, the Bahia Design Center.

DIEGO FELIX SAN MARTIN—LONNE

Diego Félix San Martín and Juan Martín Lonne became partners in 1988. Their professional standing grew after they were featured in several national and international publications, and via presentations at architecture biennials and

congresses in Buenos Aires, São Paulo, Madrid, Barcelona, and Beijing. In 1997, the Belas Arts Museum of Buenos Aires exhibited their work, including outstanding clubs, private residences, multipurpose buildings in Uruguay and Argentina, summerhouses, the Renault Argentina, the Renault Museum, and San Isidro and Borges stations for the Argentinean Coast Train service.

They received first prize for the Ciba-Geigy Labs, Kimberly Clark Argentina and Disney Argentina offices.

Their architectural style is widely known for being representative of the last two decades of the old millennium and as some of the best in South American architecture.

EMILIO SOYER NASH

Emilio Soyer Nash was born in Peru and has been working as an architect since 1964. His résumé lists many different works—some unusual houses, some public buildings, commercial centers, and hotels. He received the The Golden Hexagon prize for the best work at the Biennial of Architecture in Lima in 1969; and the Chavin prize from the National Culture Institute in 1972 for the building of 140 houses. In 1987, he received first prize in the Latin American Biennial in Chile for the 'Ajax Hispanic' building.

He was the President of the large, historical area of Barranco, Lima, has twice been a member of the School of Architects of Peru, and has enjoyed several stints as a jury member judging architectural works in private and public contests. His works are regularly published in Peruvian and Latin American magazines.

ENRIQUE BROWNE & ASSOCIATES

Enrique Browne was born in 1942. He graduated as an architect in 1965 and Master of Urban Planning in 1968—both with maximum distinction—from the Catholic University of Chile. Following this, he undertook advanced studies in the USA, England, and Japan. He has been a Fellow of the Ford Foundation, of the Social Science Research Council, and of the Guggenheim Foundation.

Enrique Browne has received various awards in competitions and Architecture Biennials including: first prize in the second and the 10th Architecture Biennial of Santiago de Chile (1979 and 1995); the 'Cubo de Acero CAYC' in the Second International Biennial in Buenos Aires (1987); the first Latin American Prize (1998); and the Silver Medal in the World Biennial of Architecture in Sofia, Bulgaria (1989). He was a finalist in the first Mies Van der Rohe Prize (Barcelona, 1998) and in the Vitrubio Prize in the first International Biennial of Arts (Buenos Aires, 2000).

He is author of three books and 60 essays on architecture and urbanism. His work has been the subject of three monographs and his projects have been featured more than 170 times in specialized international magazines.

FABRIZIO CECCARELLI

Fabrizio Ceccarelli was born in Rome and completed his architecture studies there. Since 1974, he has lived in Rio de Janeiro, and his work has mainly focused on leisure projects. The basis of his design is the spontaneous

manifestation of primitive Brazilian architecture—using local materials as a starting point—for a diverse range of structures. Wood, bamboo, sisal, straw, and many other organic materials occupy integrated spaces within the natural surrounding context. His sophisticated Italian education and Brazil's natural resources make for some very interesting and intriguing designs.

FRANZ KRAJCBERG

Franz Krajcberg was born in Poland in 1921. In 1947, with Chagal's help, he came to Brazil. He was disillusioned with human beings and shocked at the loss of his entire family in the Holocaust. He became a Brazilian citizen in 1954. Before coming to Brazil, he had studied Fine Arts and Engineering in Leningrad and had been in touch with the Bauhaus movement in Stuttgart, studying with Baumeister.

Internationally renowned, Krajcberg divides his time these days between Paris and the city of Nova Viçosa in Bahia. There, he lives in a house on top of a tree, set within 54 hectares (133.4 acres) of preserved forest.

He has traveled several times to the Amazon and taken many photographs, utilizing his capacity to see everything, especially the Amazon's exuberance, which has forced him to "face a world of continuous shapes and mutations, different from the values traditionally recognized by the modern human being." He was with Pierre Restany in 1978 in the Amazon when the journalist wrote the famous 'Manifest of Rio Negro' about aesthetic alternatives, which exactly describes the essence of Krajcberg's art. Through his transformation of wood stems, twisted branches, and the ruins of burnt forests into art, Kraj, as he is affectionately known, has won many prizes and honors during his life.

With his continued energy, he is preparing to inaugurate two museums to house his wonderful work; one in Paris and the other in Nova Viçosa.

GERSON CASTELO BRANCO

As a youngster, Gerson Castelo Branco, a native of the Brazil's northeast area, used to joke about being an architect as he performed experiments at his parent's and friends' houses. After finishing his architectural studies at the Federal University of Bahia, Castelo Branco traveled for six months through the Inca Empire in the Andes Mountains, returning to Brazil to establish his home on one of the northeast fishing beaches. Here, he undertook his first serious architectural works, creating the simple houses of the local fishing population, using local natural materials such as sisal, wood, and bamboo. With the 1977 construction of the 'Fishing House' in the shape of a sailing craft, the term 'Paraqueira Brasileira' was born, a name used by Castelo Branco to describe the totality of his works. This is his registered trademark—and he has often said, "Every work of art must have a name."

It was in Ceará that Castelo Branco established his home, and where his projects have developed their character and achieved international recognition.

He has participated in a number of expositions and architectural biennials, been awarded many prizes, and his works have been published in national and international magazines. He travels around Brazil lecturing at universities and cultural centers.

HUMBERTA FARIAS

Fascinated by space, landscape, and almost all the different artistic manifestations, Humberta Farias has one great passion: architecture. She completed her architectural studies in 1980 at the Federal University of Alagoas, and went on to postgraduate study in Brasilia. Farias then worked in various companies in São Paulo, Rio de Janeiro, and Recife before setting up her own firm. The principal things she learnt from the masters were spatial organization and an understanding of Brazil's strong social and cultural diversity.

Absorbed by aesthetic balance, environmental wellbeing, and the perfect integration of the project with nature, she achieves the contemporary, the universal, and the regional, through pure and strong forms and her trademark power to synthesize.

Her intense professional motivation reveals itself in residential projects, medical and commercial unities, and interior design. She seeks a very Brazilian architecture, based on knowledge of regional problems and the critical conscience founded on the client and local workmanship.

LÍLIAN AND RENATO DAL PIAN

Lílian Dal Pian graduated from the Faculty of Architecture and Urbanism at the University of São Paulo in 1981, and was a teacher at the Faculty of Architecture and Urbanism, at the Catholic University of Campinas in 1991 and 1995. She is a member of the Directory of the Institute of Architects of Brazil, São Paulo division.

Renato Dal Pian graduated from the Faculty of Architecture and Urbanism at the Faculty of Architecture and Urbanism at the Catholic University of Campinas in 1981 and has been a professor since 1993 at the Faculty of Architecture and Urbanism at Mackenzie University, where he received a Masters in 2002. He was a member of the Consulting Board of the 4th International Biennial of Architecture of São Paulo in 1999/2000. Both architects worked in London and Milan from 1986 to 1992.

Returning to Brazil in 1992, they established Dal Pian Arquitetos Associados in São Paulo. The firm has won several architectural contests and has been involved in residential, commercial, and industrial buildings during recent years, as well as urban projects and city planning.

MARCOS ACAYABA

Marcos Acayaba is a native of São Paulo City and he completed his architecture studies at the University of Architecture of São Paulo (FAU) in 1969. He attended several specialized courses, holds a postgraduate degree from FAU in the subject of Ambiental Urban Structures, and in 1998 he obtained his most recent qualification, a diploma on the subject of Programmed Readings in Architectural History.

He has taught at many universities throughout Brazil and, since 1994, has been Professor of Project Buildings at FAU (USP).

Acayaba has traveled widely throughout Brazil to lecture on different aspects of architecture at the invitation of universities and cultural centers. He participated in conferences at the Chile Biennial and at the Catholic University of Antofagasta (Chile) in 1997. He also traveled to Portugal in 1999 to participate in a lecture at the invitation of the ISCTE (Superior Institute of Science of Work and Business). The year 2000 saw him participating in the third International Seminar of Latin American Architecture in Cochabamba, Bolivia. He has participated in several national and international exhibitions, winning prizes on a number of occasions. In 1997, he was awarded the Grand Prize of the International Biennial of Architecture of São Paulo for the 'Acayaba House,' which is presented in this publication.

He has collaborated with a number of different architects on common projects and has also been involved in various partnerships. Since 1979, he and Marlene Milan Acayaba have been partners in Marcos Acayaba Architects S/C Ltd.

His works reflect discipline in a number of different areas including urban, public and commercial buildings, complexes, collective houses, and residential buildings, and his projects have been published in international and national publications.

MATHIAS KLOTZ GERMAIN

Mathias Klotz Germain was born in Viña del Mar, Chile, in 1965. He studied in Santiago at the Catholic University of Chile and is one of South America's most prominent young architects, last year winning the Francesco Borromini Prize for Young Architects, in Italy, for his work 'Altamira's School.' He has had wide experience as an academic, teaching Architecture at Valparaiso University since 1993 and becoming the Director of Diego Portales University in 2001. Studio Mathias Klotz and Associates, Architects has designed many different works since 1988: residential houses, commercial and industrial projects, and institutional and urban buildings. He has also taken the opportunity to broaden his artistic horizons by becoming Art Sirector for the movie 'Last Call' and the theatrical show '5 Sur.'

He has participated in various competitions and has received a number of important prizes. He has twice has been a finalist for the Mies Van Der Rohe Prize, in 1998 and 2001. His works appear frequently in national and international magazines and at expositions all over the world. At present, the Studio is designing residential projects in Denmark, Argentina, and Chile. He is also developing a circus project, a commercial building, and some urban projects in his native country.

NELSON DUPRÉ

Nelson Dupré was born in São Paulo, Brazil in April 1947, and graduated as an architect from Mackenzie University in 1973. He was the Architecture, Design and Project Manager at Botti Rubin Architects from 1972 until 1985, the year he opened his own firm, Dupré Arquitetura e Coordenação S/C Ltda. Since then, he has worked on medium, and large-scale projects, and been responsible for more than 3.5 million square meters (37.7 million square feet) of building construction, including residential and commercial buildings, banks, schools, stores, hospitals, sports centers, and theaters—for both public and private clients.

In recent years, he has concentrated more on industrial buildings and historical restoration, participating in the restoration of the São Paulo Municipal Theater and the Pedro II Theater in Ribeirão Preto. He has overseen projects for the Coca-Cola-Panamco factory in Jundiaí, the German pharmaceutical laboratories of B/Braun in Rio de Janeiro, and the American company Stiefel in São Paulo, among others.

The restoration of Julio Prestes Central Station and the construction of the São Paulo Concert Hall's main auditorium brought together all his professional experience, particularly in construction. It is without doubt his most important achievement. For this work, he received two international and four Brazilian prizes, among them the USITT (United States Institute for Theater Technology) Architecture Award 2000— Honor Award, USA, the FIABCI (Fédération Internationale des Professions Immobiliéres) Prix d'Excellence 2001—Oslo, Norway, and the IAB (Brazilian Institute of Architects) Award 2000—Hors Concurs with honor.

OCTÁVIO RAJA GABAGLIA

Octávio Raja Gabaglia was born in Rio de Janeiro and has visited Búzios regularly since the 50s. Later, he took up residence there and worked as an architect, building more than 1000 houses, mostly in that area. Always very concerned with the environment, he defends the preservation of the natural habitat of his city and uses disposable resources. He also makes extensive use of natural materials, taking advantage of tiles, beams, and whatever he can from the old colonial houses, injecting into the present day the charm of colonial Brazil. With the lack of potable water in Búzios, he has developed a peculiar system to take advantage of the ocean water. At first, this was principally for his benefit but today it is being used more and more by the city's government.

RICARDO SALEM AND BEATRIZ REGIS BITTENCOURT

Born in Rio de Janeiro, where he trained in law, Ricardo Salem is also known as a talented designer. The son of an intellectual, he was raised in an environment which encouraged the study of different disciplines. His travels took him around the world and he grew familiar with many different countries and their people—this broadened his outlook and augments his present profession of architecture and design. Tired of the kind of life he was living in Rio de Janeiro, he decided in the late 1970s to make radical changes. He changed his place of residence and lifestyle. He went to live in Bahia, in far-away Trancoso, which, until then, was only known in the Brazilian history books. With some friends, he bought land and beaches, blending the solitude and peace in Trancoso with a busy life in Rio, São Paulo, Paris, and other world centers. When he built his own house in the early 80s, he observed and studied the techniques and methods of the natives, who preserved the existing vegetation and used local materials. These methods were employed not just to facilitate the work but also to preserve the old style of life and housing, which has existed since the colony was first settled. Friends asked for houses in the same style as his own house.

Around that time he knew Beatriz Regis Bittencourt, an architect who completed what he felt was missing. They became partners with specific roles. Ricardo dealt with the client and Beatriz stayed at the drawing table putting his creativity into practice.

Beatriz was born and studied in Rio de Janeiro, and her architectural career has seen her work in different studios on different projects, from the small and handmade to the large and practical.

The two of them worked together, although each had their own studio, designs, and ideas. Beatriz, a design board professional, creates wonderful projects beyond those she shared with her partner. Ricardo, more eclectic, designs furniture and objects that have a unique Transcoso identity.

CONTACT DETAILS

ALEXIA LEÓN ANGELL
Calle Diez Canseco, 212
Oficina 202
Miraflores
Lima 18, Peru
Telephone: (51 1) 445 0500
Mobile: (51 1) 917 7709
Email:
alexialeon@terra.com.pe

ANNE MARIE SUMNER
Rua Alves Guimarães, 784
São Paulo SP, Brazil
CEP: 05410-001
Telephone/fax: (55 11) 3085
2846
Email:
ams-arquitetura@uol.com.br

**BEATRIZ REGIS
BITTENCOURT**
Alameda Sol Poente s/n
Trancoso postal address—
MCPC 06
Município de Porto Seguro
BA Brazil
CEP: 45810-000
Telephone: (55 73) 668 1154
Email: beatrizrb@uol.com.br

BORSOI & ASSOCIATES
Rua Miguel Pereira, 38
Humaitá
Rio de Janeiro, Brazil
CEP: 22261-090
Telephone/fax: (55 21) 2535
2676
Email:
borsoiecosta@uol.com.br
Rua Domingos Ferreira, 92
Pina Recife Pernambuco
Brazil
CEP: 51011-050
Email:
borsoiecostarc@uol.com.br

BOTTI RUBIN ARCHITECTS
Rua Hungria, 888—7º andar
São Paulo, Brazil
CEP: 01455-000
Telephone: (55 11) 3816 1055
Email: bra@bottirubin.com.br

**CLÁUDIO BERNARDES &
PAULO JACOBSEN**
Avenida Ataulfo de Paiva,
1351 Leblon
Rio de Janeiro, Brazil
CEP: 22441-031
Telephone: (55 21) 2512 7743
Email: bjq@bjq.com.br

DAVID BASTOS
Praça dos Tupinambás 2
Salvador, Bahia
CEP: 40015-240
Telephone: (55 71) 241 2777
Email:
davidbastos@uol.com.br

**DIEGO FELIX SAN
MARTIN—LONNE**
Paraná 759 2º Piso
Buenos Aires C.P. C1017 AAN
República Argentina
Telephone: (54 11) 4372
3938/2618/2681
Fax:(54 11) 4372 0201
Email: estúdio@sanmartin-
lonne.com.ar

EMILIO SOYER NASH
Malecón Mariscal
Castilla #176 Barranco
Lima, Peru 4
Telephone: (51 1) 247 0588
Email:
cruzdelsur@terra.com.pe

ENRIQUE BROWNE &
ASSOCIATES
Los Conquistadores 2461
Providencia
Santiago, Chile
Telephone: (56 2) 234 2027/
1397
Fax: (56 2) 231 5630
Email:
ebrowne@entelchile.net

FABRIZIO CECCARELLI
Rua São Clemente, 413
CEP: 22260-001
Rio de Janeiro, Brazil
Telephone: (55 21) 2286 5255
Email:
fabrizioceccarelli@br.inter.net

FRANZ KRAJCBERG
Sítio Natura
Nova Viçosa
Bahia, Brazil
Mobile: (55 73) 9986 0120

GERSON CASTELO
BRANCO
Rua Monsenhor Bruno, 750
Meireles
Fortaleza
Ceará, Brazil
CEP: 60115-190
Telephone: (55 85) 264 2165
Email:
gerson@ultranet.com.br

HUMBERTA FARIAS
Avenida Maceió, 36 Jaraguá
Maceió, Alagoas, Brazil
CEP: 57025-080
Telephone: (55 82) 231 8588
Email:
humbertafarias@bol.com.br

LÍLIAN AND RENATO
DAL PIAN
Avenida Higienópolis,
529 cj. 11
São Paulo, Brazil
CEP: 01238-001
Telephone: (55 11) 3822 1218
Email: dalpian@sti.com.br

MARCOS ACAYABA
Rua Helena, 170
São Paulo, Brazil
CEP: 04552-050
Telephone: (55 11) 3849 1045
Email: macayaba@uol.com.br

MATHIAS KLOTZ
GERMAIN
Isidora Goyenechea 3356
oficina 60, Las Condes
Santiago, Chile
Telephone: (56 2) 233 6613
Fax: (56 2) 232 3282
Email:
mathiasklotz@terra.com.cl

NELSON DUPRÉ
Rua Artur de Azevedo, 1466—
3º andar, Pinheiros
São Paulo, Brazil
CEP: 05404-003
Telephone: (55 11) 3088 7922
Fax: (55 11) 3088 5672
Email: duprearq@uol.com.br
Website:
www.duprearquitetura.arq.br

OCTÁVIO RAJA
GABAGLIA
Ponta da Sapata s/n
Armação de Búzios
Rio de Janeiro, Brazil
CEP: 28950-000
Telephone: (55 22) 2623 2150
Email:
rajagabaglia@uol.com.br

RICARDO SALEM
Praça São João s/n
Trancoso postal address—
MCPC 20
Município de Porto Seguro
BA Brazil
Telephone: (55 73) 668 1178
Email: rs.salem@uol.com.br

ACKNOWLEDGMENTS

It has been a privilege for The Images Publishing Group
to include the work of renowned South American
architects and photographers in this publication.
We wish to thank Sylvia Haidar for her vision,
patience and tireless effort in bringing South American
architecture to a forum for international readers.